DBT, CBT, and ACT Workbook

Behavioral Therapy Tools and Cognitive Strategies for Managing Depression, Anxiety, and Improving Mental Health

Isabelle Rivers

Table of Contents

Introduction

"My negative thoughts are suffocating me."

"Anxiety paralyzes me, I can't even leave the house."

"Even when something good happens, I can't enjoy it. I'm just waiting for the next disaster."

"My emotions are like a tornado, completely overwhelming me."

"I'm afraid I'll never overcome this depression."

"My worries are out of control, I can't stop them."

"I feel trapped in a cycle of thoughts and behaviors I can't break."

"Stress is consuming me, I don't know how to handle it anymore."

"I feel disconnected from myself and everyone around me."

If you recognize yourself in these statements, I want you to know one thing: you're not alone. I know how hard it can be to wake up every morning, hoping today will be different, that today you'll finally be able to control those intrusive thoughts, those overwhelming emotions. Maybe you start the day with good intentions, determined not to let anxiety or depression take over. But then, slowly, you feel those familiar doubts creeping in. The strategies you've always used don't seem to work anymore. You find yourself overwhelmed, trapped in a spiral of negative thoughts that seems endless. In those moments, you might wonder, "Is it really worth it? Why do I keep fighting?" And then, with a sense of dismay, you realize you're stuck again in that familiar cycle of emotional distress.

But listen closely: there's a reason you feel this way, and more importantly, there's a solution. What you're experiencing could be a mood or anxiety disorder, and there are specific therapeutic approaches that can help you. I know it might be hard to believe right now, but those mood and anxiety disorders that keep you trapped are not a life sentence. They're mental states that push you to stay stuck in thought and behavior patterns that no longer serve you, even though part of you desperately wants change. I recognize how frustrating this can be: you want an emotionally balanced and fulfilling life, but it seems that every time you try, you end up feeling overwhelmed or scared.

Perhaps you're afraid of losing control if you allow yourself to fully feel your emotions. You might believe that facing your thoughts and feelings means being overwhelmed by them. I understand. This fear is deeply rooted and often operates at a subconscious level. It manifests as irritability, intense anxiety, a sense of despair, and the desire to avoid anything that might trigger strong emotions. But I want you to know it doesn't have to be this way.

You might be wondering why you feel this way. Many people struggling with mood and anxiety disorders have experienced stressful or traumatic events, both in childhood and as adults. These experiences can lead to a deep-seated belief that the world is a dangerous and unpredictable place, and that your emotions and thoughts are uncontrollable. Does this sound familiar? Maybe you always expect the worst, or you feel you're not up to the challenges life presents. This is a protective response, a coping mechanism born out of fear and past pain. Your daily struggle could be the result of these old emotional wounds reactivating.

I know it might seem safer to avoid or fight against your inner experiences. It's an automatic response, a survival instinct that prioritizes perceived emotional safety. But in doing so, you're also giving up the chance to live a full and satisfying life. Your past experiences might have taught you that opening up emotionally is dangerous, but I assure you there's another way to live.

Do you recognize this pattern? You start new experiences or relationships full of hope and optimism. But as soon as challenges arise, you feel a sudden shift. You start seeing everything negatively or catastrophically. Doubts emerge out of nowhere, and situations that once seemed manageable now appear insurmountable. Small problems become huge obstacles. This is your "deactivation strategy" in action, a subconscious way to protect yourself from feeling overwhelmed. I know how tempting it can be to withdraw or constantly fight against these feelings. But by doing so, you're depriving yourself of the opportunity to develop true emotional resilience. You're missing out on the richness of life experiences, the joy of meaningful connections, the opportunities for personal growth.

There are several reasons why you might be afraid of losing control or being overwhelmed by your emotions and thoughts. Perhaps you believe you need to control every aspect of your emotional experience. You might feel incompetent or helpless when you can't "fix" your emotions. Or maybe you have a natural aversion to intense emotions and constantly try to escape them. You might also believe that taking care of yourself is selfish, or have a deep fear of failure that drives you to sacrifice your well-being. All these fears stem from inaccurate and deeply rooted beliefs.

At the core of all this, you might have the belief that you're unworthy of peace and happiness. The fear of getting too close to your emotions might stem from the belief that you have intrinsic flaws that will inevitably make you unhappy. But listen carefully: this is not the truth about you. These are just beliefs that can be changed. I know it might seem like an enormous task right now, but I want you to know there's hope. Mood and anxiety disorders are not a life sentence. They're patterns of thought and behavior that, with the right approach and commitment, can be transformed.

And this is where DBT, CBT, and ACT come into play. These therapies offer powerful tools to address the problems you're experiencing. Here's what you can expect to learn:

- How to challenge the false beliefs that keep you stuck and build solid self-esteem.

- How to recognize and assert your emotions, needs, and boundaries in a healthy way.

- How to manage guilt constructively instead of letting it paralyze you.

- How to cultivate and maintain positive mental health, creating a balance that works for you.

- How to identify and eliminate behaviors that hinder your well-being and relationships.

- How to develop emotional management skills that will allow you to face life's challenges with confidence.

This book is more than just a text. It's a personal guide for your journey of self-discovery and healing. Every page contains valuable insights and practical strategies that you can apply immediately in your life. I invite you to immerse yourself deeply in this content. Don't just read passively, but actively engage with the material. Try the exercises, reflect on the questions posed, and above all, be patient and kind to yourself as you embark on this journey.

Remember, you're not alone on this journey. Millions of people have faced similar challenges and have emerged stronger and more resilient. You can do it too. You've already taken the important first step by opening this book. Are you ready to discover the secrets to achieving lasting emotional well-being and the fulfilling life you deserve? Turn the page and let's begin this journey together. I can't wait to guide you through this transformation process.

PART 1 - DBT

Welcome to the Dialectical Behavior Therapy (DBT) section of our journey. DBT is a powerful approach that combines cognitive-behavioral techniques with mindfulness practices. Originally developed to treat borderline personality disorder, DBT has since proven effective for a wide range of emotional and behavioral issues. In this section, you'll learn about the core principles of DBT, including mindfulness, distress tolerance, emotion regulation, and interpersonal effectiveness. We'll explore how these skills can help you navigate intense emotions, improve your relationships, and create a life worth living. Whether you're dealing with mood swings, impulsivity, or chronic stress, the DBT tools and exercises in this section will equip you with practical strategies for achieving emotional balance and personal growth.

Chapter 1:

The Basics of DBT

"Life is a balance of holding on and letting go." - Rumi

In this chapter, you will explore the foundations of Dialectical Behavior Therapy (DBT), an innovative approach to managing intense emotions and improving interpersonal relationships. DBT offers practical tools to balance self-acceptance with the desire for change, helping you navigate life's emotional challenges more effectively.

You'll start by discovering the origins of DBT and how it has evolved over time. You'll gain an understanding of the fundamental principles that guide it, including the key concept of dialectics. You'll also explore the four main modules of DBT and how they work together to promote emotional well-being.

Whether you're dealing with anxiety, depression, relationship issues, or simply looking to improve your mental health, this chapter will provide you with a solid foundation to understand how DBT can be beneficial in your life. Get ready to discover an approach that balances compassion and change, offering you new perspectives for facing daily challenges.

Origins and Development of DBT

Dialectical Behavior Therapy (DBT) didn't emerge out of nowhere. It has a rich and fascinating history, deeply intertwined with the life and experiences of its creator, Dr. Marsha Linehan. In the 1970s, while working with patients who struggled with chronic suicidal thoughts and behaviors, Linehan became frustrated with the limitations of existing therapies and sought a more effective approach. Her brilliant insight was to combine two seemingly opposing concepts: acceptance and change.

Drawing on her training in Cognitive Behavioral Therapy (CBT), Linehan realized that CBT alone was insufficient for some patients, particularly those with Borderline Personality Disorder. These patients often felt invalidated and misunderstood, reacting negatively to immediate attempts to change their behaviors. To address this, Linehan incorporated elements of Zen philosophy, particularly the concepts of mindfulness and acceptance, providing a necessary counterbalance to CBT's emphasis on change. She also introduced the concept of dialectics, derived from Western philosophy, which in DBT involves seeing reality as a continuous flow of opposing forces, each containing elements of truth. This approach helps overcome the "all-or-nothing" thinking common in emotional disorders.

Over the years, DBT has evolved from a specific treatment for Borderline Personality Disorder into a versatile approach applicable to a wide range of emotional and behavioral issues. Today, it is recognized as an evidence-based treatment for numerous conditions, including mood disorders, anxiety disorders, eating disorders, and addictions. What makes DBT unique is its balance between scientific rigor and human compassion. Linehan emphasized the importance of treating patients with dignity and respect, validating their experiences while encouraging change.

The story of DBT is also a testament to resilience and personal transformation. In 2011, Linehan publicly revealed her own struggles with mental health issues, including suicidal thoughts in her youth. This revelation added depth to her theory and demonstrated the potential for healing and growth within each of us. As you delve into the world of DBT, remember that you are following in the footsteps of countless individuals who have found hope and healing through this approach. DBT is not just a set of techniques but a way of viewing the world and yourself with greater understanding and compassion.

Fundamental Principles of DBT

Dialectical Behavior Therapy (DBT) is built on a set of interconnected principles that form its theoretical and practical foundation. At the core of this approach lies the concept of dialectics, a way of thinking that recognizes and accepts the existence of seemingly opposing truths. This principle is evident in the delicate balance between acceptance and change that DBT promotes.

When practicing DBT, you learn to accept yourself and your current reality without judgment while also acknowledging the necessity and possibility of change. This doesn't mean resigning yourself to your situation; rather, it creates a space of understanding from which transformation can emerge. Closely tied to this concept is the practice of mindfulness. Through present-moment awareness, you observe your thoughts and emotions without being overwhelmed by them. Mindfulness in DBT goes beyond simple meditation; it becomes a way of approaching life with intentionality and presence.

Validation is another crucial element in this process. Recognizing and accepting your thoughts, feelings, and behaviors as understandable within the context of your experiences helps you build a solid foundation for change. Simultaneously, DBT teaches you to recognize and counteract invalidation, whether it comes from others or is self-inflicted. A fundamental principle of DBT is the belief that everyone is doing their best given their current circumstances. This compassionate perspective is not an invitation to complacency but a starting point for personal improvement.

DBT also emphasizes the importance of continuous learning, encouraging you to view every situation, even the difficult ones, as opportunities for growth. This ties into the idea that everything is interconnected: your thoughts influence your emotions, which in turn affect your behaviors, creating a continuous cycle. As you integrate these principles into your life, you'll find that they are not just theoretical concepts but practical tools for navigating daily challenges.

The goal of DBT is not to eliminate pain or difficulties entirely—an unrealistic expectation—but to equip you to manage challenges more effectively, allowing you to live a richer and more meaningful life despite adversity.

The Four Modules of DBT

Dialectical Behavior Therapy (DBT) is structured around four main modules, each addressing specific aspects of emotional and relational well-being: Mindfulness, Distress Tolerance, Emotion Regulation, and Interpersonal Effectiveness. Together, these modules form a comprehensive and integrated approach to managing emotional and behavioral challenges.

Mindfulness: The Foundation of DBT

Mindfulness is the first module and serves as the foundation for all other DBT skills. In this module, you learn to focus your attention on the present moment, observing your thoughts, emotions, and bodily sensations without judgment. Mindfulness practices help you increase awareness of your mental processes, reduce emotional reactivity, improve concentration, and make more intentional decisions. The mindfulness skills in DBT are divided into "What" skills (observe, describe, participate) and "How" skills (non-judgmentally, one-mindfully, effectively).

Distress Tolerance: Navigating Crises

The Distress Tolerance module equips you with tools to handle crisis situations and moments of intense emotional stress. The skills you learn in this module enable you to overcome difficult moments without making the situation worse, accept reality as it is (radical acceptance), healthily distract yourself from painful thoughts and emotions, and calm yourself during high-stress times. This module includes strategies like STOP (Stop, Take a step back, Observe, Proceed mindfully) and TIPP (Temperature, Intense exercise, Paced breathing, Progressive muscle relaxation).

Emotion Regulation: Managing Emotions Effectively

The Emotion Regulation module teaches you how to understand and manage your emotions more effectively. The goals of this module include identifying and naming emotions, understanding the function of emotions, reducing emotional vulnerability, increasing positive emotions, and decreasing the intensity of negative emotions. You learn strategies such as the ABC model (Accumulation of positive emotions, Building mastery, Coping ahead) and techniques for modifying emotions through opposite action.

Interpersonal Effectiveness: Improving Relationships

The final module, Interpersonal Effectiveness, focuses on enhancing your relationships with others. The skills you acquire in this module help you communicate assertively, maintain self-respect in social interactions, balance your needs with those of others, and build and maintain healthy relationships. This module introduces techniques like DEAR MAN (Describe, Express, Assert, Reinforce, stay Mindful, Appear confident, Negotiate) for making effective requests, and GIVE (Gentle, Interested, Validate, Easy manner) for maintaining positive relationships.

Integrating the Modules

These four modules do not operate in isolation but are interconnected and support each other. For example, mindfulness skills help you stay centered while practicing distress tolerance. Improved emotion regulation can lead to more effective interpersonal interactions, and interpersonal effectiveness can reduce stress in relationships, thereby decreasing the need for distress tolerance strategies.

Regular practice of these skills creates a synergistic effect, leading to an overall improvement in your emotional well-being and quality of life. Over time, these skills become more natural, allowing you to face daily challenges with greater resilience and flexibility. While these modules are often presented in a specific order during DBT treatment, in real life, you will frequently use them in combination. The ultimate goal is to integrate them seamlessly into your daily life, creating a holistic approach to managing emotions and relationships.

As you progress in your DBT journey, you will discover how these modules work together to provide you with a complete set of tools for navigating the complexities of emotional and relational life. Remember, consistent practice is key to mastering these skills and experiencing the lasting benefits of DBT.

Dialectics in DBT

Dialectics in DBT is a core concept that deeply influences the approach to treatment and everyday life. Essentially, it involves a way of thinking that recognizes and accepts the existence of seemingly contradictory or opposing truths. At the heart of dialectics in DBT is the balance between acceptance and change, allowing you to accept yourself as you are in this moment while also acknowledging the need and desire for change. This perspective helps you move beyond "all-or-nothing" thinking, which often fuels emotional distress.

Dialectical thinking is based on the idea that everything is interconnected, change is the only constant, and a synthesis emerges from opposing extremes. Applying this mindset to your life can transform the way you handle challenges. For instance, dialectical thinking allows you to feel an intense emotion while choosing not to act on it. You can recognize your current limitations while working to overcome them. In a discussion with a friend, you might acknowledge that both of you have valid points, even if your views seem opposed.

In DBT treatment, dialectics appears in various forms. Therapists balance validating your experiences with encouraging change, and they may use therapeutic paradoxes to spark new insights. You learn to find "wisdom" in opposing perspectives instead of seeing situations in black and white. A key concept here is radical acceptance, where you fully accept reality as it is while actively working to change it. This approach helps you navigate complex situations with greater flexibility, both in therapy and in everyday life.

By integrating dialectical thinking, you may notice increased tolerance for ambiguity and uncertainty, reduced internal and external conflicts, and an improved ability to find creative solutions to problems. This way of thinking can also lead to a deeper sense of connection with yourself and others. Dialectics in DBT is not just a theoretical concept but a practical tool for facing daily challenges. It encourages you to view situations from multiple perspectives, remain flexible in the face of change, and find a balance between apparent opposites. With practice, this approach can become a natural part of your thinking, leading to greater emotional resilience and a more balanced life.

Exercise 1: Navigating Emotional Storms

Think of an emotionally intense situation you are currently facing. Describe the situation and how you could apply the concept of dialectics to manage it.

_____

_____

_____

_____

_____

_____

_____

_____

Exercise 2: Applying DBT Modules

For each of the four DBT modules, identify a personal challenge you could address using those skills.

Mindfulness:

_____

_____

_____

_____

Distress Tolerance:

_____

_____

_____

_____

Emotion Regulation:

_____

_____

_____

_____

Interpersonal Effectiveness:

_____

_____

_____

Exercise 3: Practicing Dialectical Thinking

Reflect on a recent situation. Describe your initial thoughts, then consider an opposite perspective. Finally, find a dialectical synthesis between these two views.

Initial Thoughts:

_____

_____

_____

_____

Opposite Perspective:

_____

_____

_____

_____

Dialectical Synthesis:

_____

_____

_____

_____

By completing these exercises, you'll begin integrating DBT principles into your daily life. Remember, consistent practice is key to developing these skills.

Chapter 2:

Mindfulness - The Heart of DBT

"The present moment is the only time where life touches eternity." - Eckhart Tolle

In this chapter, you will explore the concept of mindfulness and its central role in Dialectical Behavior Therapy. You'll discover how the practice of mindfulness can transform your relationship with thoughts and emotions, providing you with a powerful tool to navigate daily challenges. You will learn specific DBT mindfulness skills and how to apply them in your life. This chapter will lay the foundation for a practice that can lead to greater emotional stability and a deeper sense of connection with yourself and the world around you.

What is Mindfulness?

In the context of DBT, mindfulness goes beyond simple meditation. It is about being fully present in the current moment, without judgment. Imagine observing the flow of your thoughts and emotions as a curious witness, without getting swept away or reacting automatically.

This practice differs from other forms of meditation due to its pragmatic focus and integration into daily life. While some traditions aim to achieve altered states of consciousness, the DBT approach teaches you to stay grounded in the present reality, enhancing your ability to handle difficult situations.

The benefits of this practice are numerous and profound. With regular exercise, you might notice:

- Greater mental clarity and concentration

- Reduced stress and anxiety

- Improved management of intense emotions

- Increased self-awareness and awareness of others

- Enhanced ability to respond rather than react to situations

This technique offers you a pause between stimulus and response. In this space, you find the freedom to choose how to act, rather than being driven by automatic reactions. This brief pause can make the difference between impulsive action and thoughtful response.

The goal isn't to eliminate negative thoughts or emotions, but to observe them without being overwhelmed. It's like watching clouds pass in the sky: you see them, acknowledge them, but you don't identify with them.

The DBT approach emphasizes practical application in daily life. It's not about sitting in meditation for hours, but about bringing a constant awareness to your daily activities. Whether you're washing dishes, talking with a friend, or dealing with a stressful situation at work, this practice helps you stay present and centered.

This exercise requires patience and consistency. Initially, you may find it challenging to maintain focus on the present moment. Your mind will wander, and that's okay. The skill lies in noticing when your mind drifts and gently bringing it back to the present, without self-criticism.

Over time, this practice can become an inner refuge, a place of calm that you can access at any moment, regardless of external circumstances. This inner resource will accompany you through life's ups and downs, offering you a sense of stability and clarity even in the most turbulent moments.

The Role of Mindfulness in DBT

Mindfulness is the cornerstone of Dialectical Behavior Therapy (DBT), influencing and enhancing every aspect of treatment. It acts as a lens that brings your present experience into sharp focus, making you more aware and capable of effectively applying other DBT skills.

In distress tolerance, mindfulness allows you to recognize early signs of discomfort, enabling you to intervene before the situation escalates. For emotion regulation, it helps you observe your emotions without being overwhelmed by them, creating the space needed to apply more effective management strategies.

Mindfulness is essential for behavioral change as it trains you to notice habitual patterns of thinking and behavior, the crucial first step toward change. By observing thoughts and behaviors without judgment, you open yourself to the possibility of making more conscious and deliberate choices.

Mindfulness also sharpens your ability to accurately identify and name your emotions. Instead of just feeling a vague sense of discomfort, you can distinguish specific nuances of anger, sadness, or anxiety. This deeper understanding allows you to respond more appropriately and effectively.

Observing emotional states without trying to change or avoid them often reduces their intensity. Additionally, recognizing the transient nature of emotions provides comfort during difficult moments and reduces the likelihood of overreacting.

In interpersonal interactions, mindfulness enhances the quality of your presence. You learn to truly listen, rather than just thinking about your next response, fostering deeper and more meaningful relationships.

The "What" Skills: Observe, Describe, Participate

To make mindfulness a tangible part of your life, DBT offers three fundamental skills: Observe, Describe, and Participate. These skills will help you better manage your emotions, reduce stress, and improve your relationships.

Observe:
This skill teaches you to pay attention to your experience without trying to change it. Imagine yourself as a scientist observing an experiment with curiosity. Notice your thoughts, feelings, and bodily sensations without judgment. You might observe the rhythm of your breath, tension in your muscles, or the thoughts crossing your mind. The goal isn't to change these experiences, but simply to acknowledge them. This practice creates space between you and your internal experiences, reducing emotional reactivity.

To practice observation:

- Focus on your breath for a few minutes each day.

- Notice physical sensations as you walk or move.

- Observe your thoughts as if they were clouds passing in the sky.

Describe:
This skill helps you put into words what you observe, without interpretations or judgments. It's like being a sports commentator who only describes what they see. Describing allows you to label your experiences, creating a useful distance between you and what you're going through. Instead of being overwhelmed by an emotion, you can say, "I'm feeling anger," or "I notice anxious thoughts." This simple act of labeling can reduce the intensity of difficult emotions.

To improve your describing skills:

- Practice using phrases like "I notice that I'm thinking..." or "I feel a sensation of..."

- Describe objects or situations objectively, without adding opinions.

- When you feel an emotion, try to describe it in terms of physical sensations.

Participate:
This skill teaches you to fully immerse yourself in the present moment, without separating yourself from the experience. It's like being a dancer who becomes one with the music. Fully participating in the present moment helps reduce anxiety about the future or regrets about

the past. It allows you to live more fully and enjoy what's happening now, rather than always being mentally elsewhere.

To practice participation:

- Engage fully in an activity you enjoy, letting go of worries.

- During a conversation, listen attentively without thinking about what you'll say next.

- When doing sports or exercise, focus entirely on the sensations in your body.

These skills work together to help you be more present and aware. Observing allows you to notice what's happening, Describing helps you understand it better, and Participating lets you fully experience the moment.

In daily life, you might use these skills in various ways. For example, in a stressful situation at work, you could first Observe your reaction (noticing tension in your body or anxious thoughts), then Describe the experience to yourself ("I'm noticing thoughts of worry and tension in my shoulders"), and finally, Participate fully in the task at hand, focusing only on what you can do in the present moment.

By practicing these skills regularly, you'll notice a significant change in how you handle stressful situations. You'll be able to respond to life's challenges with greater calm and clarity, rather than reacting impulsively. You may find it easier to manage intense emotions, improve your interpersonal relationships, and increase your productivity.

Remember, the key is consistent practice. Don't get discouraged if it seems difficult at first. Over time, these skills will become more natural and offer you a powerful tool to manage stress and live a more balanced life. Start with small moments of practice during the day and gradually increase the duration and frequency. Even just a few minutes a day can make a big difference in the long run.

The "How" Skills: Non-Judgment, One-Mindfulness, Effectiveness

After understanding what to do in mindfulness practice, it's crucial to grasp how to do it. The "How" skills—Non-Judgment, One-Mindfulness, and Effectiveness—provide the tools to deepen your practice and apply it effectively in daily life.

Non-Judgment:
This skill teaches you to observe your experiences without labeling them as good or bad. Often, we automatically judge situations, thoughts, and emotions, which adds unnecessary stress and suffering. Non-judgment allows you to see things as they are, without the filter of your evaluations.

To practice non-judgment:

- Notice when you're judging. Phrases like "should" or "shouldn't" are often indicators of judgment.

- When you catch yourself judging, simply observe the judgment without judging the fact that you're judging.

- Try to describe situations in terms of objective facts rather than subjective evaluations.

For example, instead of thinking, "This day is terrible," you might notice, "It's raining today, and I have a lot of work to do." This perspective can reduce stress and open you up to more creative solutions.

One-Mindfulness:
This skill encourages you to treat each moment as unique and new. We often approach situations based on past experiences or future concerns, losing sight of what's actually happening in the present.

To practice one-mindfulness:

- Approach each situation as if it's the first time you're encountering it.

- Pay attention to details you usually overlook in daily activities.

- When you find yourself thinking, "It's always like this" or "This will never change," remind yourself that each moment is new and different.

This practice can help you break out of negative thinking patterns and see new possibilities in familiar situations.

Effectiveness:
This skill focuses on doing what works in a given situation, rather than what you think is "right" or what you wish were true. Effectiveness helps you navigate life's challenges pragmatically.

To practice effectiveness:

- Ask yourself, "What would work best in this situation?"

- Be willing to compromise when necessary.

- Focus on what you can control, rather than what you cannot change.

For example, if you disagree with a colleague, instead of insisting on being right, you might seek a compromise solution that works for both of you.

These "How" skills work together to support and enhance the "What" skills. Non-judgment allows you to observe and describe more accurately. One-mindfulness helps you fully participate in the present experience. Effectiveness guides you in applying these skills practically in your life.

By practicing these skills, you might notice:

- A decrease in stress and anxiety, as non-judgment reduces self-criticism.

- Greater appreciation for daily experiences, thanks to focusing on the uniqueness of each moment.

- Improved problem-solving skills, through the application of effectiveness.

Remember, these skills require practice and patience. Don't expect perfection; instead, aim to gradually incorporate them into your daily routine. You might start by dedicating a few minutes each day to mindful practice, perhaps during activities like eating, walking, or brushing your teeth.

Over time, you'll find these skills becoming more natural, and you'll start applying them automatically in various situations. This can lead to greater peace of mind, more satisfying relationships, and an increased ability to handle life's challenges.

The ultimate goal is to integrate these skills so they become a way of living, not just a separate practice. When that happens, you may discover a new freedom in how you approach life, with greater flexibility, compassion, and wisdom.

Exercise 1: Mindful Observation

Choose a common object and describe it in detail, focusing only on what you can observe objectively, without judgments or interpretations. Consider aspects such as shape, color, texture, weight, and any other physical characteristics you notice. Avoid including personal opinions or emotional associations.

_____

_____

_____

_____

_____

_____

_____

Exercise 2: Practicing the 'What' Skills

For each of the 'What' skills (Observe, Describe, Participate), write a brief example of how you might apply it in a daily situation. Try to be specific and concrete in your examples.

Observe:

_____

_____

_____

_____

_____

_____

Describe:

_____

_____

_____

_____

_____

_____

Participate:

_____

_____

_____

_____

_____

_____

Exercise 3: Practicing the 'How' Skills

For each of the 'How' skills (Non-Judgment, One-Mindfulness, Effectiveness), write a brief example of how you might apply it in a challenging daily situation. Reflect on how applying these skills could change your experience of the situation.

Non-Judgment:

_____

_____

_____

One-Mindfulness:

_____

_____

_____

Effectiveness:

_____

_____

_____

Exercise 4: Mindful Experience

Choose a daily activity (such as eating, walking, or washing your hands). Perform the activity mindfully, paying full attention to every aspect of the experience. Then, describe your experience, focusing on what you noticed using your senses and how it was different from usual. Include details about what you saw, heard, touched, smelled, or tasted, and how you felt during the activity.

_____

_____

_____

Chapter 3:

Distress Tolerance

"You can't stop the waves, but you can learn to surf." - Jon Kabat-Zinn

This chapter will equip you with the tools to handle stress and crises with greater balance. You will learn to recognize warning signs, discover techniques to manage difficult moments, and explore the concept of radical acceptance.

Understanding Stress and Crises

Stress is a natural reaction to life's challenges, but it becomes problematic when it overwhelms your ability to cope. A crisis is a moment of intense stress that severely tests your emotional equilibrium and ability to function normally.

When you're stressed, your body reacts by activating the sympathetic nervous system. Your heart rate increases, muscles tense up, and breathing becomes shallow. Your mind follows suit, with thoughts racing and often focusing on negative scenarios. Concentration wanes, making it hard to make rational decisions.

Recognizing the signs of an impending crisis is crucial. Common indicators include:

- Changes in sleep or appetite
- Persistent muscle tension, especially in the neck and shoulders
- Difficulty concentrating or remembering simple details
- Physical sensations like tightness in the chest or a lump in the throat
- Recurrent, obsessive thoughts about a problematic situation
- A tendency to isolate or seek excessive reassurance

Paying attention to these signals allows you to intervene early, before the situation worsens.

Chronic stress has detrimental effects on both physical and mental health. It can weaken the immune system, increase the risk of cardiovascular disease, and exacerbate conditions like depression and anxiety. Learning to manage stress is not a luxury but a necessity.

With practice, you can train your brain to respond to stress more adaptively. The distress tolerance techniques you will learn are valuable tools for getting through acute crises, creating the space needed to address problems more effectively.

Remember, the goal is not to live a stress-free life. A certain level of stress can be motivating and stimulating. The key is to learn how to manage it so that it doesn't take control of your life.

Stress can manifest differently for everyone. Some may feel emotionally overwhelmed, while others may experience primarily physical symptoms. It's important to recognize your personal patterns of stress response.

In the following sections, you'll explore concrete strategies for handling stress and crises. You'll learn crisis survival techniques, discover the power of radical acceptance, and delve into methods of distraction and self-soothing. These tools will help you expand your stress management capabilities, enhancing your resilience in the face of life's challenges.

Crisis Survival Strategies

When you're in the midst of a crisis, it can feel like the world is collapsing around you. In these moments, you need quick and effective tools to regain control. Crisis survival strategies are techniques you can use immediately to manage acute stress and prevent impulsive actions you might regret.

STOP

- S - Stop. Halt what you're doing, don't act on impulse.

- T - Take a step back. Distance yourself from the situation.

- O - Observe. Notice what's happening inside and around you.

- P - Proceed mindfully. Move forward with awareness, choosing the wisest response.

This simple sequence gives you the time to breathe and assess the situation more clearly. Practice it regularly, even in less stressful situations, so it becomes second nature when you really need it.

TIPP

- T - Temperature. Change the temperature of your face. Immerse it in cold water or apply a cold pack.

- I - Intense exercise. Engage in short bursts of intense physical activity.

- P - Paced breathing. Practice controlled breathing, slowing your breath.

- P - Progressive muscle relaxation. Gradually relax your body's muscles.

These actions have an immediate effect on your nervous system, helping you calm down quickly. Cold water on your face, in particular, triggers the dive reflex, slowing your heart rate.

Distraction

Distraction is another crucial strategy. When you're overwhelmed by intense emotions, shifting your focus to something else can give you the space needed to regain balance. Effective distraction activities include:

- Counting objects of a certain color in the room
- Solving a puzzle or logic game
- Listening to loud music
- Taking a hot or cold shower
- Holding an ice cube in your hand

Self-Soothing

Self-soothing techniques, based on the five senses, can be particularly effective:

- Sight: Look at calming images or an object you particularly like.
- Hearing: Listen to nature sounds or your favorite music.
- Smell: Use essential oils or smell the scent of a flower.
- Taste: Slowly savor a piece of chocolate or a warm drink.
- Touch: Stroke a soft fabric or hug a pillow.

Improving the Moment

Improving the moment is another powerful strategy. You can do this through imagination, visualizing a safe and peaceful place, or by finding meaning in the difficult situation. Ask yourself, "What can I learn from this experience? How can it make me stronger?"

Remember, these strategies are not a permanent solution to underlying problems but tools to help you get through acute crises. The goal is to give yourself the time and mental space needed to face challenges more constructively.

It's important to personalize these techniques based on your preferences and needs. What works for one person may not be effective for another. Experiment with different strategies and create your own personal "crisis survival kit."

Practice these techniques regularly, not just during crises. The more you use them, the more automatic and effective they will become when you truly need them. It's like training a muscle: the more you exercise it, the stronger and more responsive it becomes.

Radical Acceptance

Radical acceptance is a powerful concept that can transform your relationship with life's difficult situations. It's not about passive resignation but an active approach that allows you to face reality as it is, without wasting energy on a futile struggle against what you cannot change.

Imagine being stuck in traffic. You could get angry, honk your horn, and curse at other drivers. Or you could accept the situation, relax, and maybe listen to music or a podcast. The traffic won't change, but your experience will be radically different.

Radical acceptance doesn't mean approving of or agreeing with a negative situation. It means acknowledging that reality is what it is at this moment, regardless of what you wish it were or think it should be. It's an act of courage that frees you from fighting the inevitable and opens up the possibility of responding constructively within the limits of the situation.

Here are some steps to practice radical acceptance:

- Acknowledge reality. Observe the facts of the situation without judgment.

- Remember that everything has a cause. Things don't happen by chance, even if we don't always understand why.

- Accept that life can be unfair. Not everything has a satisfying reason or explanation.

- Accept your emotional reaction. It's normal to feel anger, sadness, or frustration in the face of difficult situations.

- Practice acceptance with your whole being. It's not enough to say, "I accept"; you need to feel it deeply.

- Embrace willingness to do what works. Instead of fighting reality, focus on how you can respond effectively.

Radical acceptance can be particularly useful when facing:

- Irreversible losses (a ended relationship, a missed opportunity)

- Personal characteristics you cannot change (height, age, past experiences)

- Situations beyond your control (other people's behavior, natural events)

By practicing radical acceptance, you might notice that:

- Emotional pain decreases. Resisting reality often intensifies suffering.

- You have more energy to address problems. You're not wasting it fighting the inevitable.

- Your relationships improve. You accept others for who they are, not who you wish they were.

- You become more resilient. You face difficulties with greater emotional balance.

However, radical acceptance is not easy. It can be a painful process, especially at first. You might feel as though you're giving up or surrendering. But in reality, you're making room for new possibilities.

A practical exercise to cultivate radical acceptance is the "mountain meditation." Imagine yourself as a solid, immovable mountain. Seasons change, storms come and go, but the mountain remains. Likewise, you can learn to stay centered and stable in the face of life's challenges.

Radical acceptance is an act of freedom. It frees you from the struggle against what you cannot change and opens up the possibility of fully living in the present, despite difficulties. It's a path that requires courage, but it can lead to a profound transformation in your relationship with yourself and the world.

Distraction and Self-Soothing Techniques

When emotions become overwhelming, distraction and self-soothing techniques can provide a much-needed pause. These tools aren't meant to be a permanent escape but a way to buy time and create mental space, allowing you to respond wisely instead of reacting impulsively.

Distraction Techniques

Distraction can take many effective forms when you need it most. You might try mental exercises like counting and categorizing, listing items in a category alphabetically. Engaging in mental games, such as solving puzzles or Sudoku on your smartphone, can effectively shift your focus. Sensory tasks, like touching objects with different textures and mentally describing the sensations, can anchor you in the present. Visualizing a serene place, involving all your senses, can offer a mental refuge. Even a brief physical activity, such as doing a few jumps or stretches, can break the cycle of negative thoughts.

To make these techniques more accessible, consider creating a personal "distraction toolkit." This could include items like a stress ball, a coloring book with mandalas, or a playlist of interesting podcasts. The key is to choose things that resonate with you and that you can easily use in various settings.

<u>Self-Soothing Techniques</u>

Self-soothing techniques work directly on your nervous system to induce a state of calm. These often involve engaging your five senses. For sight, you might focus intently on a complex image or watch videos of natural landscapes. Hearing can be stimulated with nature sounds, relaxing music, or guided meditation apps. For smell, keep calming essential oils on hand or create a scented sachet with soothing herbs. For taste, you could slowly savor a strong candy or sip a warm tea, focusing on the sensations. Touch can be engaged by stroking a soft fabric or using a weighted blanket.

Combining distraction and self-soothing techniques can enhance their effectiveness. For example, you might color a mandala while listening to relaxing music, engaging your sight, touch, and hearing simultaneously. Or you could take a short walk focusing on the scents around you, blending physical distraction with olfactory stimulation.

It's important to intervene at the early signs of stress, before the emotion becomes overwhelming. In difficult social situations, you can use discreet techniques like controlled breathing or holding a calming object in your pocket. Using these techniques proactively, before stressful events, can help you prepare mentally.

Exercise 1: Personal Crisis Plan

Create an action plan for moments of crisis. Reflect on your past experiences and what you've learned in this chapter.

Warning Signs:

_____

_____

Distraction Strategies:

_____

_____

Self-Soothing Techniques:

_____

_____

Exercise 2: Practicing Radical Acceptance

Think of a difficult situation that you cannot change. Describe the situation, your feelings about it, and how you might practice radical acceptance in this case.

_____

_____

_____

_____

_____

_____

Exercise 3: Improving the Moment

List 5 activities or thoughts you could use to improve a difficult moment. For each, briefly explain how it could help you.

_____

_____

_____

_____

_____

_____

_____

_____

_____

_____

_____

Exercise 4: Distraction and Self-Soothing Techniques

Create your personal kit of distraction and self-soothing techniques. For each sense, note down a technique that you believe could work for you in moments of stress.

Sight:

Hearing:

Touch:

Smell:

Taste:

Now, think of two distraction activities you could use in stressful situations:

_____

_____

_____

_____

_____

Finally, briefly describe how you might combine a distraction technique with a self-soothing technique:

_____

_____

_____

_____

_____

Chapter 4:

Emotion Regulation

"The greatest weapon against stress is our ability to choose one thought over another." - William James

Emotions are an essential part of your life, but they can sometimes feel overwhelming. In this chapter, you'll explore the complex world of emotions and learn how to manage them more effectively. You'll discover how to recognize, understand, and modulate your emotions, gaining practical tools to handle stress with greater balance.

The Role of Emotions

Emotions are more than just feelings; they are powerful messengers that inform you about what's happening both within you and around you. Fear warns you of potential dangers, anger signals injustice, and joy highlights what is important to you. Without emotions, navigating life would be like steering a boat without a rudder.

However, there are common myths about emotions that can hinder your ability to manage them effectively. One such myth is that emotions are irrational and should be suppressed. In reality, emotions have their own internal logic, and ignoring them can lead to less effective decisions. Another myth is the idea that there are "good" and "bad" emotions. All emotions have a role and can be useful if understood and managed correctly. Even anger, often seen negatively, can motivate you to change unjust situations.

Emotions deeply influence your behavior and relationships. When you're happy, you tend to be more sociable and creative. When you're anxious, you might avoid situations that could actually benefit you. Unprocessed emotions can lead to overreactions or inappropriate responses, damaging your relationships with others.

Learning to recognize and manage your emotions can significantly improve the quality of your life. It allows you to make more thoughtful decisions, communicate more effectively, and build stronger relationships. It's not about rigidly controlling your emotions, but rather developing greater flexibility in your emotional responses.

Emotions are also contagious; your emotional state can affect those around you, for better or worse. Being aware of this makes you more responsible in managing your emotions, not just for your own well-being but also for the well-being of others.

Emotions are a valuable resource. Learning to work with them, rather than against them, is key to a more balanced and fulfilling life. In the following sections, you'll explore practical tools to achieve this.

Identifying and Naming Emotions

Recognizing and naming your emotions is crucial for effective emotional management. This process helps transform vague experiences into something more concrete and manageable. The act of "labeling" activates areas of the brain associated with cognitive control, allowing you to observe the emotion with greater objectivity.

Primary Emotions

Primary emotions are innate and fundamental:

- Joy
- Sadness
- Anger
- Fear
- Surprise
- Disgust

These emotions are immediate reactions to stimuli and have clear evolutionary functions. For example, fear prepares you to escape danger, while joy motivates you to repeat pleasurable experiences.

Secondary Emotions

Secondary emotions are more complex and arise as reactions to primary emotions or thoughts about them. Examples include:

- Shame
- Guilt
- Jealousy
- Pride
- Anxiety

For instance, you might feel shame (a secondary emotion) for experiencing fear (a primary emotion) in a situation where you think you shouldn't have been afraid. Recognizing this distinction is crucial. Often, secondary emotions cause more problems because they can mask or complicate the original emotion. Identifying the underlying primary emotion can help you respond more appropriately to the situation.

Techniques to Improve Emotional Awareness

- Practice mindfulness: Observe your physical and emotional sensations without judgment.

- Use an emotion diary: Regularly note what you're feeling, in what situations, and with what intensity.

- Expand your emotional vocabulary: Be more specific in describing your emotions.

- Pay attention to your body: Emotions often manifest through physical sensations.

- Reflect on your reactions: When you overreact, pause and ask yourself what you're truly feeling.

- Ask for feedback: People around you can offer valuable perspectives on your emotions.

The goal is to develop a deeper familiarity with your emotional landscape. This awareness will allow you to respond to situations more flexibly and adaptively. With practice, your emotions will become valuable guides in your life journey, rather than obstacles to overcome.

The DBT Emotion Regulation Model

The DBT Emotion Regulation Model, known as the ABC Model (Accumulation, Boiling Point, Consequences), provides a framework for understanding and managing your emotions. This approach allows you to intervene at different stages of the emotional process, giving you greater control over your experience.

Explaining the ABC Model

- Accumulation: In this stage, events and thoughts gradually build up, contributing to the intensification of an emotion. You may not be fully aware of this process until the emotion becomes more intense.

- Boiling Point: This is when the emotion reaches its peak intensity, making it feel overwhelming and difficult to manage.

- Consequences: This stage involves the actions you take in response to the intense emotion. These actions can be adaptive or maladaptive, affecting your well-being and relationships.

Factors Influencing Emotional Intensity

Several elements can amplify or reduce the intensity of your emotions:

- Physical vulnerability: Fatigue, hunger, or illness can make your emotions more intense.

- Past experiences: Similar past events can color your current emotional reaction.

- Beliefs and expectations: Your beliefs about a situation can intensify or mitigate your emotional response.

- Social environment: The context and the people around you can influence the intensity of your emotions.

- Selective attention: Focusing on certain aspects of a situation can amplify specific emotions.

Strategies for Intervening at Each Stage

- Accumulation Stage:

  - Practice mindfulness: Learn to recognize the early signs of an intensifying emotion.

  - Modify your environment: If possible, remove yourself from situations or stimuli that fuel negative emotions.

  - Self-care: Maintain a healthy routine of sleep, nutrition, and exercise to reduce emotional vulnerability.

  - Cognitive restructuring: Challenge negative or distorted thoughts that contribute to emotional buildup.

- Boiling Point Stage:

  - Grounding techniques: Use breathing exercises or focus on your senses to anchor yourself in the present.

  - Distraction: Engage in an activity that requires your attention to temporarily distance yourself from the intense emotion.

  - Self-validation: Acknowledge the legitimacy of your emotion without judgment.

  - Progressive muscle relaxation: Systematically relax muscle groups to reduce the physical tension associated with the emotion.

- Consequences Stage:

    o Reflective pause: Before acting, stop and consider the potential consequences of your actions.

    o Opposite action: Act in a way that is contrary to the impulse generated by the emotion if the impulse is unhelpful.

    o Problem-solving: Identify concrete actions you can take to address the situation constructively.

    o Assertive communication: Express your needs and feelings clearly and respectfully, without aggression or passivity.

Applying the ABC Model requires practice and patience. At first, it may be challenging to recognize which stage you're in or to apply the appropriate strategies. Over time and with practice, you'll become more skilled at identifying the early signs of emotional accumulation and intervening effectively at each stage.

Remember, the goal is not to eliminate emotions but to manage them more adaptively. Sometimes, allowing an emotion to run its natural course can be the wisest choice. Other times, early intervention can prevent excessive or harmful reactions.

The ABC Model provides a roadmap for navigating your emotional landscape. It helps you understand that emotions are not instant events but processes that develop over time. This understanding gives you more opportunities to influence the course of your emotional experiences.

As you practice these strategies, you may find that some work better for you than others. It's important to personalize your approach and be gentle with yourself in the learning process. Emotion regulation is a skill that develops over time, and every step toward greater awareness and control is a success.

Strategies for Modifying Emotions

Modifying your emotions doesn't mean suppressing or ignoring them, but rather learning to manage them in a healthy way. This allows you to respond to situations more flexibly and effectively.

Techniques for Reducing the Intensity of Negative Emotions

- Mindful Breathing: Focus on your breath, slowing and deepening it. This activates the parasympathetic nervous system, reducing stress.

- Decentering: Observe your thoughts and emotions as if you were an external spectator. This can help you distance yourself from intense emotions.

- Reframing: Look for alternative perspectives on the situation. Ask yourself, "Is there another way to view this?"

- Gradual Exposure: Gradually face situations you avoid due to negative emotions. Over time, this can reduce anxiety.

- Progressive Muscle Relaxation: Systematically tense and relax muscle groups to reduce physical tension associated with stress.

- Emotion Diary: Regularly write about your emotions. This can help you process them and identify patterns.

Strategies for Increasing Positive Emotions

- Gratitude: Spend time each day reflecting on what you're grateful for. This shifts focus from negative to positive experiences.

- Acts of Kindness: Performing acts of kindness for others can increase feelings of connection and happiness.

- Positive Visualization: Vividly imagine positive future scenarios or recall happy moments from the past.

- Pleasant Activities: Regularly schedule activities that bring you joy, even small ones.

- Social Connection: Cultivate positive relationships and seek meaningful connections with others.

- Mindfulness of Positive Experiences: When you experience something pleasant, give it your full attention, savoring it completely.

The Importance of Opposite Action

Opposite action is a powerful technique that involves acting in a way that's contrary to the impulse generated by a negative emotion. This can break harmful emotional cycles and create new positive experiences.

How to Apply Opposite Action:

- Identify the emotion and the associated impulse. For example, fear might drive you to avoid a situation.

- Assess whether the emotion is justified by the current situation or if it's a habitual reaction.

- If the emotion isn't helpful, act in the opposite way to the impulse. In the case of fear, you might gradually approach what you fear.

- Fully commit to the opposite action, not just superficially.

- Repeat the opposite action until the emotion changes.

Examples of Opposite Action:

- For Sadness: Instead of isolating yourself, seek the company of others.

- For Anger: Instead of attacking, try being kind or taking a step back.

- For Anxiety: Instead of avoiding, gradually face the feared situation.

Opposite action isn't always appropriate. Use your judgment to determine when an emotion is justified and when it might be helpful to modify it.

To make these strategies effective:

- Practice Regularly: Like any skill, emotion regulation improves with practice.

- Start Small: Apply these techniques first in less stressful situations, then gradually in more challenging contexts.

- Be Patient: Emotional change takes time. Don't be discouraged if you don't see immediate results.

- Personalize: Adapt these strategies to your individual preferences and needs.

- Combine Techniques: Often, using multiple strategies together can be more effective than just one.

- Monitor Progress: Keep track of how these strategies affect your emotional well-being over time.

These exercises will help you put into practice the emotion regulation techniques you've learned in this chapter. Take the time to complete them thoughtfully and honestly.

Exercise 1: Emotion Diary

For the next three days, record a significant emotion you experienced each day. Describe the situation, the emotion you felt, its intensity (from 1 to 10), and how you reacted.

Day 1

Date: _____

_____

_____

_____

_____

Day 2

Date: _____

_____

_____

_____

_____

Day 3

Date: _____

_____

_____

_____

_____

Exercise 2: Practicing Opposite Action

Think of an emotion that often causes you problems. Describe a typical situation where you feel this emotion, then list three opposite actions you could take instead of your usual reaction.

Situation and Emotion:

_____

_____

_____

_____

Opposite Actions:

_____

_____

_____

_____

Exercise 3: Strategies for Positive Emotions

List five activities that make you feel good or that increase your positive emotions. For each, write how you could incorporate it more often into your weekly routine.

_____

_____

_____

_____

_____

Chapter 5:

Interpersonal Effectiveness

"The most basic of all human needs is the need to understand and be understood." - Ralph G. Nichols

Interpersonal relationships are fundamental to our daily lives. This chapter will guide you through key skills to enhance your effectiveness in social interactions. You'll explore the principles of effective communication and learn practical techniques like DEAR MAN, GIVE, and FAST. These skills will help you express your needs, manage conflicts, and maintain positive relationships, ultimately improving the quality of your interactions and your overall well-being.

Principles of Effective Communication

Communication is the bridge that connects people. In both personal and professional relationships, the ability to communicate effectively can make the difference between connection and conflict, understanding and misunderstanding.

Clear and honest communication fosters trust and intimacy in relationships. It allows you to express your needs, share your thoughts and feelings, and resolve conflicts constructively. On the other hand, ineffective communication can lead to frustration, resentment, and isolation.

However, communicating effectively is not always easy. There are several barriers that can hinder this process:

- Incorrect assumptions: We often assume others understand what we mean without clearly explaining it.

- Intense emotions: When you're angry or anxious, it can be difficult to express yourself clearly and respectfully.

- Cultural or language differences: These can lead to misunderstandings if you're not aware and sensitive to them.

- Environmental distractions: Noise, interruptions, or the presence of electronic devices can compromise the quality of communication.

- Incompatible communication styles: Some people prefer direct communication, while others are more indirect.

- Fear of judgment: This can lead to withholding important information or not expressing your true feelings.

To overcome these barriers, assertive communication is a fundamental skill. Assertiveness allows you to express your thoughts, feelings, and needs clearly and respectfully, without violating others' rights.

Key principles of assertive communication include:

- Using "I" statements: "I think," "I feel," instead of generalizations or accusations.

- Being specific: Describe concrete behaviors rather than making assumptions about others' intentions.

- Active listening: Pay attention not only to words but also to tone of voice and body language.

- Expressing empathy: Acknowledge others' feelings and perspectives, even if you don't agree.

- Maintaining a calm tone of voice and open body language.

- Seeking win-win solutions: Focus on problem-solving rather than "winning" the argument.

Assertive communication stands out from both passive communication (where your needs are ignored) and aggressive communication (where you ignore others' needs). It allows you to stand up for yourself while maintaining respect for others.

By practicing these principles, you'll notice an improvement in your relationships. Effective communication not only helps you get what you need but also contributes to creating an environment of mutual respect and understanding.

DEAR MAN Skills

DEAR MAN is a powerful assertive communication technique that helps you express your needs and achieve your goals in social interactions. Each letter represents a crucial step in the communication process.

- **Describe:** Objectively describe the situation. Focus on the facts, avoiding judgments or interpretations. For example, instead of saying, "You're always late," you might say, "In the last three meetings, you've arrived 20 minutes after the scheduled time."

- **Express:** Share your feelings and opinions about the situation. Use "I" statements to avoid sounding accusatory. "I feel frustrated and unappreciated when I have to wait for a long time."

- **Assert:** Clearly state what you want. Be specific and direct. "I'd like you to arrive on time for future meetings, or let me know in advance if you'll be late."

- **Reinforce:** Reinforce your request by explaining the benefits for the other person or the positive outcomes of the change. "If we can be on time, we'll have more time to spend together, and our relationship will benefit."

- **Mindful:** Stay focused on your goal. Don't get distracted by attempts to change the subject or by provocations. If necessary, gently repeat your request.

- **Appear confident:** Show confidence through your body language and tone of voice. Maintain eye contact, speak with a firm and clear voice, and keep an upright posture.

- **Negotiate:** Be willing to find a compromise. Listen to the other person and seek solutions that work for both of you. "I understand traffic can be unpredictable. Maybe we could agree to notify each other if we expect to be more than 10 minutes late."

Practical Examples of DEAR MAN in Various Contexts:

- At Work:
  - Describe: "I've noticed that in the last two projects, I haven't been included in the initial planning meetings."
  - Express: "I feel excluded and concerned that I can't fully contribute to the project."
  - Assert: "I'd like to be included in these meetings from the start."
  - Reinforce: "My participation could bring new ideas and help prevent problems later on."

- In a Romantic Relationship:
  - Describe: "Lately, we've spent little time together without distractions like phones or TV."
  - Express: "I miss the deep connection we used to have."
  - Assert: "I suggest we dedicate at least an hour a day to talk without interruptions."
  - Reinforce: "This will help strengthen our bond and make us feel closer."

- With a Friend:

- o Describe: "In the past few months, you've canceled our plans at the last minute several times."

- o Express: "I feel disappointed and wonder if our friendship is still a priority for you."

- o Assert: "I'd like us to stick to our plans unless there's a real emergency."

- o Reinforce: "This will help us keep our friendship strong and enjoy our time together."

When and How to Apply DEAR MAN:

DEAR MAN is particularly useful in situations where:

- You need to make an important request.

- You need to establish clear boundaries.

- You want to resolve a conflict constructively.

- You need to negotiate a compromise.

To apply DEAR MAN effectively:

- Prepare in advance: Think about what you want to say and how to say it.

- Choose the right time: Make sure the other person is available to listen.

- Stay calm: If you feel overwhelmed, take a break and return when you're more composed.

- Be willing to listen: DEAR MAN isn't a monologue but the beginning of a dialogue.

- Practice: Like any skill, DEAR MAN improves with practice.

Remember that DEAR MAN doesn't guarantee you'll always get what you want, but it significantly increases your chances of being heard and understood. Even if you don't immediately achieve your goal, you're still building more open and respectful communication.

Regular use of DEAR MAN can lead to more satisfying relationships, increased self-confidence, and better conflict resolution skills. With practice, it will become a natural part of your communication style, allowing you to express your needs clearly and respectfully in various life situations.

GIVE Skills

While DEAR MAN helps you get what you want, GIVE teaches you how to maintain and enhance your relationships. This technique focuses on creating a positive and respectful atmosphere during interactions.

- **Gentle:** Be gentle in your approach. Avoid attacks, judgments, or sarcastic tones. Use respectful language and a calm tone of voice. Gentleness doesn't mean being weak; it means creating a safe space for communication.

- **Interested:** Show genuine interest in the other person. Listen actively, ask relevant questions, and demonstrate that you value what the other person is saying. Authentic interest fosters connection and mutual understanding.

- **Validate:** Acknowledge and validate the other person's feelings and opinions, even if you don't agree. Validation doesn't mean approval; it means recognizing the other person's experience. Phrases like "I can see why you might feel that way" can work wonders.

- **Easy manner:** Maintain a relaxed and open attitude. Use humor when appropriate, smile, and try to lighten the mood. A relaxed approach can reduce tension and make the conversation flow more smoothly.

Applying GIVE can transform the quality of your relationships. It creates an atmosphere of respect and openness, where people feel heard and appreciated. This leads to greater trust, empathy, and depth in your relationships.

GIVE is particularly useful in various situations:

Resolving Conflicts: When facing a disagreement, GIVE can help you maintain a constructive tone. Imagine discussing household chores with your partner:

- Gentle: "I'd like to talk about how we manage the chores at home. How can we find a solution that works for both of us?"

- Interested: "What do you think about the current situation? Are there tasks you prefer to do?"

- Validate: "I understand that you're often tired after work. It's normal to want to rest."

- Easy manner: "Maybe we could turn some of the chores into a fun activity we do together?"

Building Work Relationships: GIVE can improve collaboration with colleagues and supervisors:

- Gentle: Instead of harshly criticizing a mistake, you could say, "I noticed some discrepancies in the report. Can we review it together?"

- Interested: During a meeting, show interest by asking, "What challenges did you encounter on this project?"

- Validate: If a colleague expresses frustration, respond with, "It sounds like this issue is really weighing on you. It's understandable given the pressure we're under."

- Easy manner: Use a light tone to suggest an idea: "How about we try a slightly unconventional approach to solve this problem?"

Strengthening Friendships: GIVE can deepen your personal connections:

- Gentle: Instead of reprimanding a friend for being late, you could say, "I'm glad you're here now. In the future, I'd appreciate it if we could be more punctual."

- Interested: Show curiosity about your friend's interests: "You mentioned your new hobby. Tell me more about it—it sounds fascinating!"

- Validate: If a friend shares a concern, respond with, "I can see why this situation worries you. It seems really complicated."

- Easy manner: Use humor to lighten a serious conversation: "Well, at least we'll have a good story to tell from this absurd situation!"

GIVE isn't a magic formula, but a guide for creating more positive and meaningful interactions. With practice, these behaviors will become natural, leading to deeper and more satisfying relationships in every area of your life.

FAST Skills

FAST is a technique that helps you maintain self-respect in social interactions, balancing your needs with those of others. This skill is crucial for avoiding compromises that undermine your values or self-esteem.

- **Fair:** Be fair to both yourself and others. Treat yourself with the same respect you give to others. Avoid constantly sacrificing yourself or demanding more than what is reasonable. In a discussion, consider both perspectives and seek solutions that are fair for everyone involved.

- **Apologies (no excessive):** Apologize when necessary, but avoid excessive apologies. A sincere apology can repair a relationship, but apologizing too often or for things you're not responsible for can diminish your value in the eyes of others and yourself. Acknowledge your mistakes, but don't feel guilty for having needs or opinions.

- **Stick to values:** Hold firm to your values and beliefs. Don't compromise what you believe in to please others or avoid conflict. Being consistent with your values boosts self-esteem and earns the respect of others, even if they don't agree with you.

- **Truthful:** Be honest in your interactions. Truth builds trust and respect, both toward yourself and in your relationships with others. Avoid lies, exaggerations, or omissions that can compromise your integrity. Honesty also means being authentic about your feelings and needs.

Self-respect is fundamental in social interactions. When you respect yourself, you communicate to others how you expect to be treated. This not only enhances the quality of your relationships but also enables you to handle difficult situations with greater confidence and assertiveness.

Balancing your needs with those of others is a delicate art. FAST helps you find this balance:

- Recognize that your needs are just as important as those of others. Don't always put yourself second.

- Clearly communicate your needs and boundaries. Others can't respect boundaries they're not aware of.

- Be willing to negotiate, but not at the cost of your core values.

- Practice empathy, striving to understand others' perspectives without losing sight of your own.

- Learn to say "no" when necessary, respectfully but firmly.

Examples of Applying FAST:

In the Workplace: Your boss asks you to work over the weekend, but you have important plans with your family.

- Fair: "I understand the importance of the project, but I have a family commitment this weekend."

- Apologies: Don't apologize for having a life outside of work.

- Stick to values: "My family is a priority for me."

- Truthful: "I could put in some extra hours next week to make up for it."

In a Personal Relationship: A friend continues to ask for loans without repaying them.

- Fair: "I've noticed there have been several loans that haven't been repaid. We need to find a solution that works for both of us."

- Apologies: Don't apologize for bringing up the issue.

- Stick to values: "Honesty and financial responsibility are important to me."

- Truthful: "I feel uncomfortable continuing to lend money under these conditions."

Using FAST regularly can help you maintain your self-respect while also fostering healthy, respectful relationships with others. By standing firm in your values and being honest about your needs, you can navigate social interactions with confidence and integrity.

The following exercises will help you practice the interpersonal effectiveness skills you've learned in this chapter. Take the time to reflect and complete each exercise thoughtfully.

Exercise 1: Dear Man

Think of a request you would like to make to someone. Use the DEAR MAN structure to plan how you will communicate this request.

Describe:	
Express:	
Assert:	
Reinforce:	
Mindful:	
Appear confident:	
Negotiate:	

Exercise 2: GIVE

Describe a difficult situation with another person. Then, for each component of GIVE, write how you might apply it in that situation.

Situation	
Gentle:	
Interested:	
Validate:	
Easy manner:	

Exercise 3: FAST Self-Assessment

Reflect on a recent social interaction. Evaluate how you maintained your self-respect using the FAST criteria. For each component, rate yourself from 1 to 5 and write a brief comment.

Fair: 1   2   3   4   5

Comment:

_____

_____

_____

Apologies: 1   2   3   4   5

Comment:

_____

_____

_____

Stick to values: 1   2   3   4   5

Comment:

_____

_____

_____

Truthful: 1   2   3   4   5

Comment:

_____

_____

_____

Chapter 6:

Dialectics in Relationships

"Peace is not absence of conflict, it is the ability to handle conflict by peaceful means." -
Ronald Reagan

This chapter explores how to apply dialectical thinking to your interactions, offering tools to navigate conflicts and build deeper connections. You'll learn to balance acceptance and change, manage disagreements constructively, and practice mutual validation.

Understanding Dialectics in Interactions

In relationships, dialectics manifest as the coexistence of seemingly opposite truths. Think of someone you love deeply: there are probably aspects of their character that you adore and others that irritate you. Both perceptions are real and valid simultaneously—this is dialectics in action.

Dialectical thinking in relationships allows you to embrace human complexity. Instead of labeling people or situations as "good" or "bad," you recognize the nuances. Your brother can be both generous and selfish, depending on the context. Your partner can love you deeply while also needing their own space.

Accepting these contradictions doesn't mean resigning yourself to problematic behaviors; rather, it provides a broader and more flexible perspective. When you recognize that a person can have contrasting qualities, you become better equipped to address conflicts without demonizing the other person.

The "both/and" approach replaces the "either/or" mindset in relational thinking. You don't have to choose between understanding and assertiveness—you can be both understanding and assertive. A relationship doesn't have to be perfect or disposable—it can have coexisting positive and negative aspects.

This approach enriches your interactions, allowing you to see others in their entirety, with both strengths and flaws. It reduces the tendency to idealize or demonize, paving the way for more authentic and mature relationships.

Dialectics in relationships also extend to your self-perception in relation to others. You can be independent and still need connection. You can love someone and occasionally feel anger or frustration toward them.

Applying dialectics to relationships takes practice. Start by observing your reactions when you disagree with someone. Do you notice a tendency to view the situation in black and white? Challenge yourself to find the truth in both perspectives.

This way of thinking doesn't eliminate conflicts, but it transforms them. Instead of viewing disagreements as threats, you see them as opportunities for deeper understanding. Dialectics allow you to maintain connection even when opinions diverge.

Embracing dialectics in relationships doesn't mean being indecisive or lacking values. On the contrary, it enables you to hold firm to your principles while remaining open to others' perspectives. It's a delicate balance, but one that can create more resilient and fulfilling relationships.

Balancing Acceptance and Change in Relationships

In relationships, striking a balance between acceptance and change is crucial. Accepting others involves recognizing the present reality, creating a safe space for change to occur. Often, this acceptance fosters change more effectively than insistence or criticism.

To encourage change, focus on specific behaviors. Say, "I've noticed you're often late to our appointments" instead of "You're always late." This separates the behavior from the person's identity, making them more receptive to feedback.

Use open-ended questions to prompt reflection: "How do you think your lateness affects our plans?" This encourages the other person to consider the consequences of their actions.

Validation is essential in this process. Acknowledge the other person's feelings and experiences, even if you don't share their perspective. Saying, "I understand that you have a lot on your plate and that managing time can be tough," shows that you are listening and respectful.

Change takes time. Be patient and recognize small progress. If your partner makes an effort to be on time, even if they don't always succeed, appreciate their effort.

Set clear boundaries. Communicate your expectations and needs assertively: "Punctuality is important to me. How can we find a solution that works for both of us?"

Practice self-reflection. Ask yourself whether you're trying to change the other person for their benefit or your own. Often, the change we want in others reflects something we need to address in ourselves.

Use active empathy. Consider what might make change difficult for the other person. What could be their fears or resistances?

Nonviolent communication is an effective tool. Express your feelings and needs without accusing: "I feel frustrated when you're late because I need to feel respected. How can we solve this together?"

Remember that you can only control your actions. Focus on what you can change in yourself and in your approach to the relationship.

Sometimes, acceptance means recognizing that a relationship isn't healthy. In these cases, the change might involve reconsidering your involvement in the relationship itself.

Balancing acceptance and change is a skill that improves with practice, leading to more authentic and fulfilling relationships.

Managing Conflicts with a Dialectical Approach

Conflicts are inevitable in relationships, but a dialectical approach can turn them into opportunities for growth and mutual understanding. Instead of viewing disagreements as threats, see them as gateways to deeper knowledge of yourself and the other person.

Start by recognizing that both sides can have valid points. This perspective shifts the focus from "winning or losing" to "understanding and resolving." Ask yourself: "What can I learn from this situation? How can this conflict improve our relationship?"

To find a synthesis in conflicts, use the "both/and" technique. Instead of focusing on differences, look for common ground. For example, in a discussion about family finances, you might say, "I see we both want financial security. You prefer saving, and I lean toward strategic investments. How can we combine these approaches?"

Practice active listening. In conflicts, it's easy to focus on your argument and miss the other person's perspective. Make a conscious effort to truly listen. Repeat what you've heard in your own words to ensure you've understood correctly.

Use open-ended questions to explore underlying motivations. Often, surface conflicts hide deeper concerns. Asking, "What worries you most about this situation?" can reveal fears or unmet needs that weren't initially obvious.

When at an impasse, use dialectics to find a "third way." Instead of getting stuck between two opposing positions, seek a solution that incorporates elements of both. This may require creativity and flexibility from both sides.

Remember, conflict isn't just about the immediate issue but also about how you communicate and manage differences. Use conflict as an opportunity to improve your communication and problem-solving skills.

Practice "radical validation." Even if you disagree with the other person's position, you can still validate their feelings and experiences. Saying, "I understand why you're frustrated in this situation. It makes sense given your experience," can de-escalate tension.

Pay attention to your body language and tone of voice during conflicts. Non-verbal communication can escalate or de-escalate a conflict just as much as your words.

If the conflict becomes too intense, don't hesitate to take a break. Set a time to resume the discussion once both of you have calmed down. Use this time to reflect on the situation from a broader perspective.

Not all conflicts have an immediate solution. Sometimes, the wisest resolution is agreeing to disagree while maintaining mutual respect. This in itself is a dialectical act: accepting differences while preserving connection.

After resolving a conflict, take time to reflect on what you've learned. How can you apply these lessons to future situations? This approach turns every conflict into an opportunity for personal and relational growth.

Managing conflicts with a dialectical approach requires practice and patience. Over time, you'll find that this method not only resolves immediate issues but also strengthens the foundation of your relationship, creating a deeper and more resilient connection.

Self-Validation and Validation of Others

Validation is key in healthy relationships. By validating yourself and others, you create an environment of acceptance and understanding that fosters personal growth and deep connection. In relationships, validation communicates that the other person's feelings and experiences are understandable and legitimate. This doesn't mean you always have to agree, but you acknowledge the validity of their emotional experience. When people feel validated, they are more open to dialogue and change.

Self-validation is equally important. While external validation is often sought, learning to validate yourself makes you more resilient and less dependent on others' approval. Start by acknowledging your feelings without judgment. If you feel angry or sad, accept these emotions as a natural part of your experience.

To practice self-validation, speak to yourself kindly. Instead of criticizing yourself for a mistake, try saying, "It's natural to feel disappointed. I did my best with the information I had at the time." This approach allows you to learn from experiences without being too hard on yourself.

Observe your thoughts and feelings with curiosity rather than judgment. Ask yourself, "What is this emotion telling me? What do I need right now?" This practice enhances your emotional awareness and helps you respond more effectively to your needs.

When validating others, active listening is crucial. Give your full attention when someone is speaking, and try to understand their perspective. Use phrases like "I can see why you feel that way" or "It makes sense that you're frustrated in this situation."

Validation doesn't always mean agreement. You can acknowledge someone's feelings without sharing their opinion. For example, "I see how this situation has hurt you, even though I see it differently."

To validate others without compromising your values, focus on the emotional experience rather than specific actions. If a friend acted in a way you disapprove of, you might say, "I understand you felt overwhelmed and reacted instinctively, even if I don't agree with what you did."

Use "mirroring" to show active listening. Repeat key words or phrases the other person uses, demonstrating that you've paid attention and are trying to understand.

Remember, validation isn't about giving advice or trying to "fix" the situation. Often, people just need to feel heard and understood. Resist the urge to offer immediate solutions unless they explicitly ask for them.

Practice validation in everyday situations. A simple "I understand you're stressed about this deadline" can make a big difference to a colleague under pressure.

Finally, be patient with yourself as you develop these skills. Validation, like many relational skills, improves with practice. Over time, it will become a natural part of your interactions, enriching your relationships and deepening your understanding of yourself and others.

Exercise 1: Identifying Dialectics

Think of an important relationship in your life. Identify three dialectics or apparent contradictions present in this relationship.

_____

_____

_____

_____

_____

_____

_____

Exercise 2: Validation Practice

Describe a situation where you and another person have differing opinions. Write how you could validate the other person's viewpoint while maintaining your own.

Situation:

_____

_____

_____

_____

_____

Validation Practice:

_____

_____

_____

_____

_____

_____

_____

_____

_____

_____

_____

_____

_____

Exercise 3: Dialectical Synthesis

Think of a recent conflict. Briefly describe your viewpoint and the other person's perspective. Then, try to find a synthesis or a "third way" that incorporates elements of both perspectives.

My viewpoint:

_____

_____

_____

_____

_____

_____

The other person's viewpoint:

_____

_____

_____

_____

_____

_____

Synthesis:

_____

_____

_____

_____

_____

Chapter 7:

DBT and Crisis Management

"In the middle of difficulty lies opportunity." - Albert Einstein

Emotional crises can strike anyone, often unexpectedly. This chapter equips you with tools to recognize the early signs of a crisis and manage it effectively, helping you create a personal safety plan and engage your support system, transforming crises into opportunities for growth and resilience.

Identifying the Signs of an Impending Crisis

Emotional crises rarely arrive without warning, and recognizing early signs can be crucial. These signs often manifest in three areas: emotions, thoughts, and physical sensations. Emotionally, you may notice intensified feelings like anger, anxiety, or sadness that seem disproportionate to the triggering situation. Thought patterns may become more negative or catastrophic, with rigid beliefs like "I'll never make it" or "everything is pointless." Physically, your body might signal a crisis through muscle tension, changes in appetite or sleep, increased heart rate, or difficulty breathing.

Self-monitoring is essential for identifying these signs. Keeping a daily journal of your emotions, thoughts, and physical sensations helps you spot recurring patterns and triggers. Over time, you'll recognize your personal warning signs of a crisis. Create a personal alert system based on these signs, including a checklist of symptoms and assigning severity levels to each. This allows you to quickly assess your emotional state and decide when to activate coping strategies.

Involve those close to you in your alert system by explaining the signs they should watch for and how they can support you. Sometimes, others may notice changes in your behavior before you do. Regularly review and update your personal alert system, as crisis signs can vary and evolve over time.

Distinguish between normal mood fluctuations and true crisis signals. Not every moment of stress or sadness requires emergency intervention; the key is observing the intensity, duration, and impact of symptoms. Use technology to track your mood and symptoms, providing objective data on your emotional patterns. Be mindful of external factors like work stress, relationship conflicts, seasonal changes, or anniversaries of traumatic events, as these can increase crisis risk. Awareness of these factors helps you prepare and implement preventive strategies.

Quick Intervention Strategies

In the midst of an emotional crisis, having quick intervention strategies can make a significant difference. DBT offers several effective techniques for managing intense emotional distress.

Advanced Crisis Management Techniques

- Cognitive Grounding: When you feel overwhelmed, anchor your mind in the present. Name five things you see, four things you can touch, three things you hear, two things you smell, and one thing you can taste. This exercise disrupts the flow of negative thoughts and brings you back to the present moment.

- Strategic Use of Self-Talk: Create a personalized self-encouragement phrase, such as "I can handle this moment" or "This feeling will pass." Repeat it like a mantra during the crisis. With practice, this affirmation will become an emotional anchor during difficult times.

- Dual Focus Technique: While dealing with intense emotions, simultaneously focus on a neutral or pleasant activity. For instance, mentally describe a serene landscape while managing the stressful situation. This divides your attention, reducing the intensity of the negative experience.

Creating an Effective Personal Crisis Plan

- "If-Then" Approach: Identify specific crisis scenarios and plan concrete responses. For example, "If I feel overwhelmed by anxiety, then I'll take five deep breaths and call a friend." This method reduces decision-making stress during a crisis.

- Cognitive Defusion: Incorporate techniques to distance yourself from negative thoughts. Imagine your thoughts as leaves floating down a stream, watching them pass without holding on. Or, repeat a distressing thought in a silly voice to diminish its emotional power.

- Physical Self-Care: Include concrete actions to meet basic physical needs. Drinking a glass of water, having a nutritious snack, or taking a short walk can have a surprisingly positive impact on your emotional state.

Innovative Elements for Your Crisis Plan

- Sensory Anchors: Prepare a box with items that positively stimulate your senses: a comforting photo, a soft fabric, a calming scent. Using these items during a crisis can provide immediate comfort and help you regain a sense of calm.

- Temporal Restructuring: When in the midst of a crisis, challenge the belief that it will last forever. Ask yourself, "How will I feel in an hour? Tomorrow? Next week?" This exercise reminds you of the temporary nature of crises.

- Personalization Based on Interests: Include strategies that reflect your interests and strengths. If you love music, create an emergency playlist. If art calms you, keep drawing materials handy. The most effective plan is one that resonates with your unique personality.

Personal Safety Plan

A personal safety plan is an essential tool for managing emotional crises. This plan provides you with a structured guide to follow when you feel overwhelmed, helping you stay safe and regain control. Here's how to create an effective and personalized safety plan.

Essential Components of a Safety Plan

- Warning Signs: Start by identifying your personal signals that indicate an approaching crisis. These might include changes in sleep, appetite, mood, or thoughts. List them in order of severity, from the mildest to the most severe.

- Coping Strategies: Create a list of techniques that have helped you in the past. Arrange them by ease of application, starting with the simplest (such as deep breathing) and progressing to more challenging ones (such as contacting a professional).

- Emergency Contacts: List the phone numbers of trusted people, therapists, and support lines. Ensure these contacts are easily accessible, perhaps saving them on your phone under a name that makes them immediately identifiable.

- Safe Environments: Identify places where you feel safe and calm. These might be spaces in your home, a local park, or a trusted friend's house.

- Reasons to Live: Include a list of reasons why it's worth pushing through the difficult moment. These could be loved ones, future goals, or simply experiences you want to have.

Personalizing the Plan

Your safety plan should reflect your unique needs. Consider these aspects:

- Specific Triggers: Reflect on your personal triggers and include targeted strategies to address them. If you know certain environments or situations cause you stress, plan ahead on how to manage them.

- Sensory Preferences: If you have specific soothing techniques that work for you, such as listening to a particular song or touching a specific object, be sure to include them in the plan.

- Personal Resources: Think about your strengths and the resources available to you. If you have artistic skills, you might include drawing as a coping strategy. If you have a pet, consider how interacting with them might help you calm down.

- Adapting Over Time: Your plan should be a living document. Regularly review and update the plan based on your experiences and what you find most effective.

Sharing the Plan

Sharing your safety plan with trusted people is crucial for several reasons:

- Informed Support: Those close to you will be better equipped to help if they know your plan. They can remind you of strategies when you're struggling and act in line with the plan.

- Accountability: Sharing the plan creates a sense of accountability. Knowing that others are aware of your commitment can motivate you to follow through during tough times.

- Plan Enhancement: Trusted individuals can offer perspectives and suggestions you might not have considered, enriching your plan.

- Emergency Preparedness: In situations where you might not be able to communicate effectively, those who know your plan can act quickly to assist you.

- Strengthening Relationships: Sharing your plan can deepen your relationships, creating a sense of trust and openness with loved ones.

When you share your plan, clearly explain how you would like people to respond in different situations. Discuss boundaries and preferences, ensuring that the support you receive aligns with your needs.

Engaging Your Support System

Having a reliable support network can be the key to managing and overcoming crises. Building and maintaining this network requires effort, but the emotional benefits are significant. Begin by identifying those in your life who can offer support—family, friends, colleagues, and mental health professionals. Don't limit yourself to current relationships; consider joining support groups, online communities, or social activities to widen your network. Keep these connections strong by staying in regular contact, showing interest in their lives, and offering support when needed.

Asking for help can be difficult, but it's important to recognize when you need it—whether you're feeling overwhelmed, stuck in negative thoughts, or struggling with everyday tasks. When reaching out, be clear about what you need, and choose a suitable time to ask. Understand that those who support you have their own limits and may not always be available immediately.

Balancing independence with the support you receive is essential. The help you get from others should enhance your own efforts, not replace them. Set clear boundaries about how others can assist you and what you prefer to handle on your own. Be assertive: say "no" when the help offered isn't what you need, and "yes" when it is. While relying on your support network is valuable, remember to take responsibility for your well-being and be open to feedback. Show appreciation for the help you receive, but don't feel obligated to repay every kindness—expressing your thanks is enough. Support relationships will naturally change over time, so be ready to adjust your approach as needed.

Exercise 1: Crisis Signal Map

List your key signs of an impending crisis in three categories: emotions, thoughts, and physical sensations.

Emotions	Thoughts	Physical Sensations

Exercise 2: Quick Intervention Plan

Create a quick action plan to use during moments of crisis. Include 3 STOP techniques and 3 TIPP strategies that you find most effective.

STOP:

_____

_____

TIPP:

_____

_____

Exercise 3: Support Network

Identify 3-5 people who can be part of your support network. For each person, fill in the table with their name, how they can help you, and when to contact them.

Name	How They Can Help	When to Contact

Chapter 8:

DBT for Specific Issues

"The only way out is through." - Robert Frost

DBT, originally developed to address specific challenges, has proven its effectiveness across a range of issues. In this chapter, we'll explore how DBT skills can be adapted to address problems like Borderline Personality Disorder (BPD), eating disorders, anger management, and addiction.

DBT for Borderline Personality Disorder

Marsha Linehan developed DBT with a focus on the unique challenges of Borderline Personality Disorder (BPD), such as emotional instability, impulsive behaviors, and relationship difficulties. DBT techniques are tailored to address these specific issues:

Emotional regulation focuses on early identification of the signs of emotional instability typical of BPD. Patients learn to recognize the initial signs of intense emotion before it becomes overwhelming, allowing them to intervene early and prevent uncontrollable emotional escalations.

Distress tolerance skills are customized to manage the self-destructive impulses common in BPD. Techniques like "riding the emotional wave" are taught to help patients resist the urge to act impulsively during crises. Patients learn to tolerate discomfort without resorting to harmful behaviors like self-harm.

Interpersonal effectiveness focuses on managing the fear of abandonment and the oscillation between idealization and devaluation in relationships. Patients learn to maintain stable connections despite emotional fluctuations. Work is done on assertiveness and the ability to express needs and set boundaries in a healthy way.

Validation is emphasized to counteract the chronic invalidation often experienced by individuals with BPD. Patients are taught to recognize and accept their emotional experiences as valid, even when they are intense. This reduces the sense of "being wrong" and improves self-esteem.

Case studies highlight the effectiveness of this approach. Melanie, 28, significantly reduced her self-harm episodes after six months of therapy, also improving her relationships and job stability. She learned to identify emotional triggers and use self-soothing techniques instead of resorting to self-harm.

Andy, 35, learned to manage intense anger and impulsive behaviors, reporting greater emotional stability and more lasting relationships after a year of therapy. Mindfulness techniques helped him create a pause between emotion and action, allowing him to make more thoughtful choices.

Research confirms these positive outcomes: a longitudinal study showed that 75% of patients no longer met the criteria for a BPD diagnosis after two years of DBT treatment. These patients reported significant reductions in suicidal behaviors, self-harm, and hospitalizations.

DBT's approach, which emphasizes the balance between acceptance and change, proves particularly effective in treating the complexities of BPD. Patients learn to accept their intense emotions as valid while simultaneously working to develop more adaptive ways to manage them. This balance helps reduce the shame and inadequacy often associated with the disorder.

DBT for Eating Disorders

DBT provides essential tools to address dysfunctional behaviors and thoughts related to eating, helping you develop a healthier relationship with food and your body. Let's explore how to apply these skills practically.

Mindfulness and Mindful Eating:

Mindfulness helps you tune into your physical and mental sensations related to food. Before each meal, take a moment to sit quietly and breathe deeply. Notice any thoughts that arise about the food and observe the sensations in your body. Ask yourself, "Am I eating out of physical hunger or to cope with an emotion?" During the meal, chew slowly and focus on the taste, texture, and smell of the food, recognizing when you are fully satisfied. This approach helps you reestablish a genuine connection with your body's natural signals, reducing episodes of automatic or emotional eating.

Crisis Management:

Crises related to eating disorders can be intense and challenging to manage. It's crucial to have an action plan ready for these moments. Identify in advance the times of day or situations that might trigger dysfunctional behaviors, such as coming home after a stressful day. Prepare a list of alternative activities that can distract you from food-related thoughts, like taking a walk, calling a friend, or engaging in a creative hobby. Include self-soothing strategies in the plan, such as wrapping yourself in a soft blanket or taking a warm bath, which can provide comfort without relying on food. Remember, the goal isn't to avoid food altogether but to reduce the impulse to use it as your sole means of emotional regulation.

Emotional Regulation:

Eating disorders are often linked to difficulties in managing emotions. Start keeping an emotion diary where you note not only what you eat but also how you feel before, during, and after meals. This will help you identify emotional patterns that lead to dysfunctional eating behaviors. For instance, you might notice that you binge when you feel anxious or isolated. Once you've identified these patterns, work on developing more effective emotional regulation strategies, such as breathing exercises, muscle relaxation techniques, or light physical activities, which allow you to manage emotions without turning to food.

Interpersonal Effectiveness in Food-Related Situations:

Social situations involving food can be particularly stressful for those with an eating disorder. To handle these situations, prepare some assertive responses in advance that you can use when receiving comments about your physical appearance or eating habits. For example, if someone comments on your plate, you could calmly reply, "I prefer not to talk about my eating habits, thank you." Also, work on assertiveness to express your dietary needs in social situations, like asking for smaller portions or bringing a dish that makes you feel comfortable. Finally, identify people in your social circle who understand your struggles and with whom you can speak openly. Having someone you trust nearby during meals can help you feel more supported and less judged.

DBT for Anger Management

Anger is a powerful and often misunderstood emotion that can become destructive if not managed properly. DBT offers valuable tools to recognize, understand, and handle anger in a healthy way. Let's explore how you can apply these techniques to your daily life, focusing specifically on aspects related to anger management.

Mindfulness to Recognize Anger Triggers

Beyond general mindfulness practices, here are some specific techniques for managing anger:

- "Anger Thermometer": Visualize a thermometer ranging from 0 to 100. Throughout the day, pause regularly and assess your level of anger on this scale. This helps you recognize when your anger is starting to rise, allowing you to intervene early.
- Observing Angry Thoughts: When you notice angry thoughts, mentally label them as "angry thoughts" without trying to change or judge them. This detachment can reduce their power over you.
- Anger Body Scan: Focus specifically on the areas of your body where you tend to feel anger (e.g., clenched fists, tight jaw). Practice relaxing these areas several times a day.

Emotion Regulation Techniques for Anger

- Rewind Technique: When an event triggers your anger, imagine mentally rewinding the scene like a movie, slowing down and noting every detail. This can help you identify the exact point where the anger began and find alternative ways to respond.
- "Roots of Anger": Anger often masks other, more vulnerable emotions. When you feel angry, ask yourself, "What's underneath this anger? Fear? Sadness? Disappointment?" Recognizing the underlying emotion can help you manage it more effectively.
- Expressive Writing: Spend 10 minutes writing freely about your anger without censoring yourself. Then, reread what you wrote to look for patterns or insights.
- Energy Transformation: Instead of suppressing the energy of anger, find constructive ways to channel it. You might direct it into creative activities like painting or positive actions like volunteering.
- "Opposite Challenge": When you feel angry, challenge yourself to do something completely opposite to what your anger urges you to do. If you want to shout, speak in a whisper. If you want to hit something, perform a kind gesture.

Interpersonal Effectiveness in Conflict Situations

- Role Reversal Technique: In a conflict, mentally put yourself in the other person's shoes. How would they view the situation from their perspective? This exercise can broaden your perspective and reduce the intensity of your anger.
- Nonviolent Communication: Use the format: "When [specific action], I feel [emotion] because [need]. Would you be willing to [specific request]?" This approach helps you express your feelings without blaming.
- "Validation Pause": Before responding in a conflict, take a moment to find a way to validate the other person's experience, even if you don't agree with their actions.
- "Ideal Future" Technique: During a conflict, ask yourself, "How would I ideally like this situation to be resolved?" Then, consider what actions you can take now to move closer to that outcome.
- Curiosity Practice: Instead of reacting with anger, try approaching the conflict with genuine curiosity. Ask questions to better understand, such as, "Can you help me understand what led you to this conclusion?"

DBT for Addiction Management

Addictions present a complex challenge where destructive behaviors intertwine with intense emotions and dysfunctional thoughts. DBT offers valuable tools to help you navigate this struggle, enabling you to build a life worth living without relying on harmful substances or behaviors.

Adapting DBT Skills for Addictive Behaviors

In the fight against addictions, DBT skills take on specific nuances:

- Mindfulness of Cravings: When you feel the urge to use a substance or engage in an addictive behavior, observe this craving as if you were a scientist. Notice where you feel it in your body, how it changes over time, without judging or trying to suppress it. This approach can reduce the craving's power over you.

- Addiction-Proof Distress Tolerance: Create a list of distraction activities that are incompatible with your addictive behavior. For example, if you struggle with alcoholism, include activities like swimming or driving, which you cannot do under the influence of alcohol.

- Emotion Regulation and Triggers: Identify the emotions that typically precede your addictive behavior. Develop specific strategies to manage these emotions without resorting to addiction. For instance, if social anxiety drives you to drink, practice breathing techniques or use positive affirmations before social situations.

- Interpersonal Effectiveness in Recovery: Practice communicating your recovery needs. Learn to refuse offers of substances or ask for support assertively. You might say, "I appreciate the invite, but I'm in recovery and can't drink tonight. I'd still love to spend time with you in another way."

Strategies for Managing Cravings and Preventing Relapse

- Craving Surfing: Visualize your craving as a wave. Instead of fighting it, imagine riding it. Observe how it builds, peaks, and then inevitably subsides.

- Skills-Based Relapse Prevention Plan: Create a detailed plan that includes which DBT skills you will use in high-risk situations. For example, "If I feel tempted at a party, I'll use the STOP technique, call my sponsor, and practice deep breathing for 5 minutes."

- Cognitive Restructuring of Addiction-Related Thoughts: Learn to recognize and challenge thoughts that justify use. If you find yourself thinking, "Just once won't hurt," counter it with, "That's the addiction talking. I know from experience that once can lead to a full relapse."

- Gratitude Practice in Recovery: Each day, write down three things you are grateful for in your addiction-free life. This will help maintain your motivation and remind you why recovery is important.

Integrating DBT with Recovery Programs

DBT can be effectively integrated with other recovery approaches:

- DBT and 12-Step Programs: Use DBT skills to manage the emotions that arise during work on the 12 steps. For instance, mindfulness can assist during the moral inventory, while distress tolerance skills can support you in the process of admission and making amends.

- Skills Training Groups Specific to Addiction: Join groups that teach DBT skills specifically adapted for the challenges of addiction. Here, you can share experiences and strategies with others in recovery.

- Using Dialectics in Recovery: Practice accepting your history of addiction while actively working toward change. Accept that addiction will always be part of your story, but it does not have to define your future.

- Mindfulness and Relapse Prevention: Incorporate mindfulness practices into your daily recovery rituals. This can increase your awareness of triggers and improve your ability to make conscious choices.

Exercise 1: Personalizing DBT Skills

Identify a specific issue you are currently facing. Choose three DBT skills you've learned so far and describe how you could adapt them specifically for this issue.

Issue:

Skill:	Skill:	Skill:
Adaptation:	Adaptation:	Adaptation:

Exercise 2: Challenges and Solutions

List three specific challenges you encounter related to your main issue. For each challenge, write a solution based on a DBT skill.

Challenge	DBT Skill Solution

Exercise 3: Progress Diary

Use this table to track your progress in applying DBT skills to your specific issue over the course of a week.

Date	Skill Used	Situation	Outcome

Chapter 9:

Integrating DBT into Everyday Life

"We are what we repeatedly do. Excellence, then, is not an act, but a habit." - Aristotle

This chapter will guide you in transforming DBT skills from theoretical concepts into everyday practices. You'll explore strategies for applying these skills across various aspects of your life, navigating any challenges that may arise. The goal is to make DBT a natural part of your daily routine.

Generalizing DBT Skills

Bringing DBT skills from therapy sessions or textbooks into the real world takes practice and creativity. Start by identifying daily situations where DBT skills could be beneficial. For example, if you tend to overreact to criticism at work, use mindfulness skills to observe your reactions without judgment, creating a pause between the stimulus and your response.

To overcome barriers in using these skills, anticipate challenges. If you tend to forget to use techniques when stressed, set visual reminders. A post-it on your desk with the word "Breathe" can remind you to practice mindful breathing during tense moments.

Consistent practice is key. Focus on one DBT skill each day for a week. You might dedicate a week to practicing distress tolerance, using the STOP technique whenever you feel overwhelmed. The next week, shift to emotion regulation, regularly monitoring and naming your emotions.

Adapt the skills to fit your specific context. In a hectic work environment, brief moments of mindfulness during coffee breaks or between meetings can be helpful. At home, try incorporating interpersonal effectiveness skills in conversations with your partner or children.

Remember, generalizing these skills takes time and patience. Don't expect immediate perfection. Each time you apply a DBT skill in a real-life situation, you're strengthening new neural pathways and building positive habits.

Share your experiences with others who practice DBT. Joining support groups or talking with friends familiar with these techniques can provide fresh ideas on how to apply the skills creatively.

Leverage technology to your advantage. Apps can help you track your mood and remind you to practice DBT skills. Some people find it useful to set random phone alerts as reminders to do a quick mindful check-in throughout the day.

Finally, celebrate your successes, no matter how small. Each time you use a DBT skill in a challenging situation, you're making progress on your personal growth journey. Acknowledging these moments will motivate you to keep practicing.

Creating a DBT Routine

Incorporating DBT skills into your daily life requires a systematic approach. Start by identifying key moments in your day where you can integrate these practices. Begin your morning with a short mindfulness meditation as you wake up. While making your coffee, practice sensory awareness by noting the aroma, the sound of the machine, and the warmth of the cup.

During your commute, whether driving or using public transport, practice distress tolerance. If you're stuck in traffic, use the STOP technique to manage frustration—breathe deeply, observe your reactions, and choose a more adaptive response.

At work, incorporate mindful breaks between tasks. Before starting a significant task, take a minute to center your attention and set an intention. In interactions with colleagues, apply interpersonal effectiveness skills by practicing active listening and assertive communication.

To remind yourself to use these skills, create visual triggers in your environment. A small object on your desk can serve as an anchor for mindfulness. Set discreet alarms on your phone or computer as reminders to check in emotionally throughout the day.

In the evening, take time for reflection and emotional regulation. Review your day, noting moments where you successfully used DBT skills and areas for improvement. This reflection helps consolidate learning and plan for the next day.

Before bed, practice a brief body scan or meditation to relax and prepare your mind for restorative sleep. This time can also be an opportunity for gratitude, acknowledging positive aspects of your day.

As you establish this routine, balance structure with flexibility. Avoid being overly rigid, as it can lead to frustration when things don't go as planned. Be open to adapting your practice to the changing circumstances of daily life.

Start small, focusing on one or two practices until they become stable habits before adding more. This gradual approach increases the likelihood of long-term success.

Personalize your routine based on your needs and preferences. If you're more productive in the morning, focus on more demanding practices then. If specific situations regularly trigger intense emotional reactions, plan to use particular DBT skills in advance.

Involve those close to you in your practice. Let family and friends know about your commitment to integrating DBT into your life. Their support can be invaluable, and they might even be interested in learning and practicing with you.

Facing Challenges with DBT

Identifying Common Difficult Situations and Planning DBT Responses: Analyze your typical week, focusing on recurring moments of stress or conflict. These might include:

- Stressful work meetings: Before the meeting, spend 2 minutes on mindful breathing. Focus on your breath, noting the inhalation and exhalation. During the meeting, use the "steady hands, calm mind" technique. Place your hands firmly under the table, using this feeling of stability as an anchor for your attention.

- Family conflicts: Implement the "empathetic pause." When you feel tension rising, take a mindful break. Breathe deeply and imagine the other family member's perspective. What might they be feeling? What unspoken concerns might they have?

- Social anxiety: Before social events, use the "5-4-3-2-1" technique. Identify 5 things you see around you, 4 sounds you can hear, 3 things you can touch, 2 smells you notice, and 1 taste in your mouth. This exercise anchors you in the present, reducing anticipatory anxiety.

- Anger management in traffic: Create a "traffic mantra" like "Inhale calm, exhale tension." Repeat it rhythmically when you feel frustrated in traffic.

- Insomnia and racing thoughts: Develop a "mental download" routine before bed. Spend 10 minutes writing down all the thoughts worrying you, then practice the "calm lake meditation," visualizing your thoughts as leaves floating on a tranquil lake.

Strategies for Maintaining DBT Practice During Stressful Times:

- "Micro-DBT doses": Integrate brief practices into transition moments during your day. For example, take three deep breaths while waiting for the elevator or practice 30 seconds of mindfulness while standing in line at the store.

- "DBT anchor": Choose a daily object as a reminder for DBT practice. It could be your watch, a specific pen, or a bracelet. Whenever you notice or use it, do a quick mindful check-in.

- "DBT buddy system": Find a practice partner, a friend or colleague interested in personal growth. Set up a support system, sending each other encouraging messages during stressful moments or sharing brief reflections on your DBT practices.

- "DBT emergency kit": Prepare a list of your top 3 DBT skills for acute stress. It could include square breathing, self-validation, and positive distraction. Keep this list in your wallet or as your phone background for quick access during crises.

- "DBT rituals": Create small DBT rituals to incorporate into your daily routine. For example, before checking emails in the morning, spend 1 minute setting a mindful intention for the day.

- "DBT visual": Create a vision board or mind map of your favorite DBT skills. Hang it in a visible place in your home or office as a constant reminder and source of inspiration.

Using Setbacks as Learning Opportunities:

- "Relapse autopsy": After a setback, analyze the sequence of events like an impartial detective. Identify the exact point where you could have applied a DBT skill. What triggered the relapse? What warning signs did you overlook?

- "Positive reframing": Instead of viewing the setback as a failure, label it as a "learning experiment." Ask yourself: "What did I discover about myself and my triggers through this experience?"

- "Plan update": Use the insights gained from the setback to strengthen your DBT plan. Add new triggers to your awareness list or adjust strategies that didn't work as expected.

- "Imagined practice": Spend time mentally reliving the relapse situation, this time imagining successfully applying DBT skills. Visualize in detail how you could have responded differently. This visualization helps reinforce new neural and behavioral patterns.

- "Growth journal": Keep a journal dedicated to your DBT setbacks and successes. For each setback, note not only what went wrong but also what you learned and how you'll apply this lesson in the future.

- "Reflective sharing": If comfortable, share your relapse experience with your DBT support group or a trusted friend. Often, articulating the experience out loud can lead to new insights and perspectives.

- "Compassion practice": After a setback, actively practice self-compassion. Talk to yourself as you would to a dear friend who's had a setback. Recognize that setbacks are a normal and valuable part of the learning and growth process.

Maintenance and Relapse Prevention

Consolidating DBT skills requires a personalized and innovative approach. Here are advanced strategies for maintaining progress and preventing relapse:

Progress Monitoring:

- Interaction Analysis: Briefly record your significant daily interactions, assessing how you applied DBT skills. This helps identify patterns in your relationships and emotional management.

- Energy Tracking: Monitor your energy levels in relation to using DBT skills. You may find that certain practices energize you, while others are better suited for low-energy moments.

- Video Review: Periodically record a short video of yourself explaining how you're applying DBT in your life. Reviewing these over time can offer a unique perspective on your progress.

Long-Term Maintenance Plan:

- DBT Projects: Undertake personal projects that incorporate DBT principles. For example, you could create a podcast on mindfulness or start a book club focused on emotional regulation themes.

- DBT and Career: Explore how DBT skills can enhance your professional life. You might propose a workshop on effective communication based on DBT principles in your workplace.

- DBT Retreats: Plan short personal "DBT retreats," dedicating a weekend each quarter to fully immerse yourself in practice and reflection.

Strategies for Overcoming Relapses:

- Protective Factor Analysis: After a relapse, instead of focusing solely on what went wrong, identify the factors that prevented you from falling into even more problematic behaviors. Strengthen these "protective factors."

- Mental Contrasting Technique: Vividly imagine how your life will be in a year if you continue practicing DBT, then compare it with a scenario where you abandon the practice. Use this contrast as motivation.

- Therapeutic Storytelling: Write the "story" of your relapse as if you were a character in a novel. This narrative distance can provide new perspectives and insights.

- Advice to Future Self: Write a letter to your "future self" who might face a relapse, offering compassion, wisdom, and concrete strategies based on your current experience.

Exercise 1: DBT Routine Map

Use the table below to map out your typical day, identifying at least 8 moments when you can integrate specific DBT skills.

Time of Day	DBT Skill to Apply

Exercise 2: Overcoming Obstacles

Identify three common obstacles you encounter in applying DBT skills in daily life. For each, develop a strategy to overcome it.

Obstacle:

Strategy:

_____

_____

_____

_____

Obstacle:

Strategy:

_____

_____

_____

_____

Obstacle:

Strategy:

_____

_____

_____

_____

Exercise 3: Maintenance Plan

Create a weekly maintenance plan for your DBT practice. Include daily activities, weekly reviews, and strategies for handling potential setbacks.

	Daily Practice	Weekly Review	Anti-Relapse Strategy
Monday			
Tuesday			
Wednesday			
Thursday			
Friday			
Saturday			
Sunday			

PART 2 - CBT

As we move into the Cognitive Behavioral Therapy (CBT) section, we'll focus on the powerful connection between your thoughts, feelings, and behaviors. CBT is one of the most widely researched and effective forms of psychotherapy, used to treat a variety of mental health issues including depression, anxiety, and more. In this part, you'll learn how to identify and challenge negative thought patterns, develop healthier cognitive habits, and change behaviors that may be holding you back. We'll explore specific CBT techniques for different issues, from managing depression to building self-esteem. The exercises in this section will help you become more aware of your thought processes and give you practical tools to reshape your cognitive landscape for better emotional well-being.

Chapter 10:

Foundations of CBT

"The greatest discovery of my generation is that human beings can alter their lives by altering their attitudes of mind." - William James

This chapter explores the fundamentals of Cognitive Behavioral Therapy (CBT). You'll learn how thoughts influence emotions and behaviors, using this awareness to improve daily life. The origins, key principles, and application of CBT to various psychological challenges are covered.

Origins and Development of CBT

CBT has its roots in 20th-century psychology. In the 1960s, American psychiatrist Aaron Beck noticed that his depressed patients often had recurring negative thoughts, leading him to develop a therapeutic approach focused on modifying dysfunctional thought patterns. Simultaneously, Albert Ellis developed Rational Emotive Behavior Therapy (REBT), a precursor to CBT, arguing that interpretations of events, rather than the events themselves, cause distress. Both approaches differed from the dominant psychoanalysis of the time by focusing on the present, emphasizing conscious thoughts, and being structured and goal-oriented.

By the 1970s and 1980s, CBT had gained popularity for its effectiveness in treating depression. Books like *Feeling Good* by David Burns helped make CBT accessible to the public. Over time, CBT evolved, incorporating elements from other therapies and adapting to a wider range of disorders. Variations like Mindfulness-Based Cognitive Therapy (MBCT) and Acceptance and Commitment Therapy (ACT) integrate mindfulness with cognitive-behavioral principles.

A key feature of CBT is its commitment to research and empirical validation, demonstrating effectiveness across a variety of psychological disorders. Its practical, problem-focused approach contrasts with psychodynamic therapies that delve deeply into the past. CBT focuses on the present and future, providing concrete tools to modify problematic thoughts and behaviors in daily life.

CBT's collaborative nature involves working with the therapist as a team to identify and change thoughts and behaviors contributing to problems, making you an active participant in the process. Understanding and modifying the interconnectedness of thoughts, emotions, and behaviors allows for positive changes in life, offering a strong foundation for self-improvement and stress management.

In summary, CBT is an evidence-based, present-focused, and action-oriented therapeutic approach. Its evolution and proven effectiveness have made it one of the most widely practiced and studied forms of therapy worldwide.

The Cognitive Model

The cognitive model, central to CBT, revolves around the thoughts-emotions-behaviors triangle, illustrating how these three elements are tightly interconnected and continuously influence one another. Picture the triangle with "Thoughts" at the top, "Emotions" at the bottom left, and "Behaviors" at the bottom right. Each side represents the connection between two elements, where thoughts influence emotions and behaviors, emotions affect thoughts and behaviors, and behaviors, in turn, influence thoughts and emotions.

To understand this concept better, consider a common scenario: you're waiting for an important phone call. If you think, "They've probably decided not to call me," you might feel anxious or disappointed (emotion) and might avoid checking your phone (behavior). This behavior could then reinforce the initial thought, creating a negative cycle.

Thoughts play a crucial role in this model. Often, it's not the events themselves that cause your emotional reactions but your interpretations of these events. Returning to the phone call example, if you think, "Maybe they're just running late," you might feel calmer and more patient, leading to more relaxed behavior.

Your interpretations of events are shaped by your core beliefs—deep-seated thought patterns formed through life experiences. These beliefs act as filters through which you interpret the world. For instance, if you hold a core belief like "I'm not good enough," you might interpret constructive feedback at work as harsh criticism, triggering negative emotions and defensive behaviors.

The importance of interpretations and core beliefs can't be overstated. They form the lens through which you view yourself, others, and the world. Negative or distorted beliefs can lead to misinterpretations of situations, generating disproportionate emotions and counterproductive behaviors.

CBT aims to identify and modify these dysfunctional interpretations and beliefs. By learning to recognize and challenge your automatic thoughts, you can begin to change your emotional and behavioral responses.

A key aspect of the cognitive model is its cyclical nature. A change in any element of the triangle can influence the other two. For example, by modifying a behavior (like exercising regularly), you can positively affect your thoughts ("I'm doing something good for myself") and emotions (a sense of accomplishment and well-being).

The cognitive model also explains the maintenance of psychological problems. Negative thoughts can lead to distressing emotions, which may induce avoidance behaviors. These behaviors, though providing short-term relief, often reinforce the initial negative thoughts, creating a cycle that perpetuates the problem.

Understanding this model gives you a powerful tool for self-reflection and change. By paying attention to your thoughts, you can identify recurring patterns and begin to challenge them. This process of self-observation and questioning thoughts is the first step toward cognitive restructuring, a key technique in CBT.

It's important to note that the cognitive model doesn't suggest that all problems are "in your head." It acknowledges the impact of external factors but emphasizes the role of your interpretations in determining your responses to these factors.

By applying the cognitive model in your daily life, you can develop a greater awareness of your thought processes and their impact on your emotional and behavioral well-being. This awareness is the starting point for making positive and lasting changes in how you think, feel, and act.

Core Principles of CBT

Automatic thoughts are one of the key concepts in CBT. These quick, spontaneous thoughts cross your mind in response to specific situations or stimuli. Often, these thoughts go unnoticed, yet they deeply influence your emotions and behaviors.

Imagine walking down the street, and a friend passes by without acknowledging you. An automatic thought might be, "They're ignoring me; they must be angry with me." If left unchecked, this thought could lead to feelings of anxiety or sadness, affecting how you behave toward that friend later.

Automatic thoughts are often distorted or irrational. They tend to reflect negative or dysfunctional thinking patterns that have developed over time. Common examples include catastrophizing (always imagining the worst), personalization (taking responsibility for external events), and all-or-nothing thinking (seeing situations in extreme black-and-white terms).

Recognizing these automatic thoughts is the first step toward change. CBT teaches you to become more aware of these fleeting thoughts, "catch" them, and critically examine them. This process of self-observation may initially be challenging, but with practice, it becomes more natural.

The importance of evidence and reality-testing plays a crucial role in CBT. Once you've identified an automatic thought, the next step is to test it against reality. This involves gathering evidence for and against the thought, considering alternative perspectives, and assessing the likelihood of your predictions.

Returning to the example of the friend who didn't greet you, you might ask yourself, "What evidence do I have that they're ignoring me? Are there other possible explanations? Perhaps they were distracted or didn't see me?" This critical examination often reveals that your automatic thoughts aren't as accurate or realistic as they initially seemed.

Reality-testing helps you develop a more balanced and realistic perspective on situations. Instead of passively accepting your automatic thoughts as truth, you learn to view them as hypotheses to be tested. This evidence-based approach is essential for reducing the emotional impact of negative and irrational thoughts.

Cognitive restructuring is the culmination of this process. It involves actively modifying your dysfunctional thought patterns, replacing them with more balanced and realistic alternatives. This isn't about simply thinking positively but rather about developing a more flexible and adaptive way of thinking.

The process of cognitive restructuring begins with identifying negative automatic thoughts. Then, you examine these thoughts using specific questions:

- What evidence supports this thought?

- Is there evidence against this thought?

- Are there alternative explanations?

- What's the worst-case scenario? The best-case scenario? The most realistic scenario?

- What are the consequences of thinking this way?

- How would I advise a friend in a similar situation?

Through this process, you learn to generate more balanced alternative thoughts. For example, instead of thinking, "I'm a total failure because I made a mistake," you might restructure the thought to, "I made a mistake, but that doesn't define my worth. I can learn from this experience and improve."

Cognitive restructuring requires practice and patience. Initially, it may feel artificial or forced, but over time, it becomes more natural. The goal isn't to eliminate all negative thoughts but to develop the ability to respond to them in a more adaptive way.

An important aspect of cognitive restructuring is its focus on action. It's not just about changing your thoughts but using these new thoughts as a foundation for changing your behaviors. For instance, after restructuring an anxious thought about socializing, you might challenge yourself to attend a social event you would have otherwise avoided.

CBT also emphasizes the importance of testing new thoughts through direct experience. This "behavioral experiment" allows you to gather real evidence that either supports or refutes your thoughts, reinforcing the cognitive change process.

Remember, cognitive restructuring isn't about eliminating all negative emotions or seeing the world through "rose-colored glasses." The goal is to develop a more realistic and flexible way of thinking that enables you to face life's challenges more effectively and with less emotional stress.

By applying these core CBT principles—recognizing automatic thoughts, reality-testing, and cognitive restructuring—you can begin to transform your thinking and, consequently, your emotional and behavioral well-being. This process requires commitment and consistent practice, but it can lead to significant and lasting changes in your life.

Applications of CBT

CBT has proven effective in treating a wide range of psychological disorders, making it one of the most widely used therapeutic approaches. Disorders that respond particularly well to CBT include:

- Anxiety disorders (such as panic disorder, social phobia, and generalized anxiety disorder)

- Depression

- Obsessive-compulsive disorder

- Post-traumatic stress disorder

- Eating disorders

- Insomnia

- Substance abuse disorders

CBT has also shown effectiveness in treating physical problems with psychological components, such as chronic pain management and irritable bowel syndrome.

In everyday life, CBT principles can be applied to enhance overall well-being and stress management. You can use CBT techniques to:

- Improve self-esteem and self-confidence

- Manage work or academic stress

- Resolve interpersonal conflicts

- Overcome creative blocks or procrastination

- Improve sleep and eating habits

- Manage anger or other intense emotions

For example, you might use cognitive restructuring to address negative thoughts before a job interview or apply CBT problem-solving techniques to manage family conflicts.

While clinical CBT and self-help CBT share fundamental principles, they differ significantly in application:

Clinical CBT:

- Conducted by a qualified therapist

- Offers a personalized approach based on your specific needs

- Provides structured and regular support

- Can address more complex or severe issues

- Includes professional assessment and progress monitoring

Self-help CBT:

- Based on resources such as books, apps, or online courses

- Offers flexibility in learning and applying techniques

- More accessible and often less expensive

- Requires a high level of motivation and self-discipline

- Can be effective for mild or moderate issues

Self-help CBT can be a great starting point or a complement to traditional therapy. However, for more serious or persistent problems, the guidance of a professional remains invaluable.

Regardless of the approach chosen, the effectiveness of CBT largely depends on your active participation. Regular practice and applying techniques in daily life are crucial for achieving lasting results.

Remember, CBT is not a quick fix but a process of learning and change. With commitment and perseverance, you can develop skills that will be useful well beyond the end of a formal therapeutic course, providing you with valuable tools to face future challenges with greater resilience and awareness.

Exercise 1: Identifying Automatic Thoughts

Describe a recent situation that triggered a strong emotion. Identify the automatic thoughts you had in that situation and the associated emotion.

_____

_____

_____

_____

_____

_____

_____

Automatic Thoughts	Associated Emotion

Exercise 2: CBT Triangle

Think of a problem you're facing. Use the CBT triangle model to analyze it, identifying the thoughts, emotions, and behaviors involved.

Problem:

_____

_____

_____

Thoughts:

_____

_____

_____

Emotions:

_____

_____

_____

Behaviors:

_____

_____

_____

Exercise 3: Challenging Thoughts

Choose a negative automatic thought you identified. Use CBT questions to challenge it: What evidence supports and contradicts this thought? Are there alternative explanations?

Negative Automatic Thought:

_____

_____

Evidence Supporting:

_____

_____

_____

Evidence Against:

_____

_____

_____

Alternative Explanations:

_____

_____

_____

_____

_____

_____

_____

Chapter 11:

Identifying Dysfunctional Thoughts

"What we think, we become." - Buddha

Your thoughts shape your reality more than you might realize. This chapter delves into identifying the dysfunctional thoughts that impact your well-being. You'll learn to recognize the power of your inner language, common cognitive distortions, and deeper thought patterns. This exploration will equip you with tools to better understand your mind and pave the way for positive change.

The Role of Language in Dysfunctional Thinking

The internal language you use forms the lens through which you view the world. The words you choose to describe your experiences not only reflect your thoughts but actively shape them. Consider how your perception of a situation changes when you label it as "a disaster" instead of "a challenge."

Your inner dialogue acts as a constant filter, coloring every experience. Phrases like "I'll never make it" or "I'm a failure" are not just fleeting thoughts but powerful statements that influence your emotional state and future actions. The labels you assign to yourself and others have a profound impact. Calling yourself "stupid" for an occasional mistake can become a self-fulfilling prophecy, affecting your confidence and future performance. Similarly, categorizing others as "enemies" or "untrustworthy" can lead to defensive behaviors that harm relationships.

To become more aware of your inner dialogue, try this exercise: for a day, note down the phrases you frequently tell yourself. You may be surprised by the frequency and impact of certain expressions. Notice how these words affect your mood and decisions.

Another effective technique is "linguistic perspective shifting." When facing a difficult situation, try describing it as if you were talking to a friend. Often, the language we use with others is kinder and more constructive than the language we use with ourselves.

Pay attention to your use of modal verbs like "must," "should," and "can't," as they can reveal limiting beliefs. Replacing "I must" with "I choose to" can transform a perceived obligation into a conscious decision, giving you a sense of control.

Language can also be a powerful tool for change. Reframing negative statements into more neutral or positive ones can open up new possibilities for thought and action. For example, changing "I'm terrible with numbers" to "Math is challenging for me, but I can improve with practice" creates room for growth.

The goal isn't to eliminate negative language entirely but to become more aware of how your words influence your thoughts and feelings. This awareness is the first step toward a more balanced and constructive inner dialogue.

The 10 Cognitive Distortions

Cognitive distortions are distorted thinking patterns that influence your perception of reality. Recognizing them is crucial for developing more balanced thinking. Here are the 10 most common cognitive distortions:

1. All-or-Nothing Thinking: You see situations in black and white, with no shades of gray.

   o Example: After making a mistake at work, you think, "I'm a total failure."

   o Impact: This distortion leads to unrealistic standards and excessive self-criticism.

2. Overgeneralization: You draw broad conclusions from a single event.

   o Example: After a bad date, you conclude, "I'll never find love."

   o Impact: It limits your future expectations and may lead to avoiding new experiences.

3. Mental Filter: You focus selectively on negative details, ignoring the positives.

   o Example: You receive many compliments on a presentation but dwell on the one critical comment.

   o Impact: This distorts your overall view of situations, fueling negativity.

4. Disqualifying the Positive: You dismiss positive experiences, insisting they "don't count."

   o Example: When you receive a compliment, you think, "They're just being nice."

   o Impact: It maintains a negative self-view and resists positive change.

5. Jumping to Conclusions: You make negative assumptions without sufficient evidence.

- Mind Reading: You assume you know what others are thinking.
  - Example: "I know my boss thinks I'm incompetent."
- Fortune Telling: You predict things will turn out badly.
  - Example: "I'm definitely going to fail the exam."
- Impact: These unfounded assumptions can influence your behavior and create self-fulfilling prophecies.

6. Magnification or Minimization: You exaggerate the importance of certain events while downplaying others.
   - Example: You blow your mistakes out of proportion and minimize your successes.
   - Impact: This creates a distorted perception of your abilities and the value of your experiences.

7. Emotional Reasoning: You assume your feelings reflect reality.
   - Example: "I feel stupid, so I must be stupid."
   - Impact: This can lead to decisions based on temporary emotions rather than objective facts.

8. "Should" Statements: You impose rigid rules on how you should behave.
   - Example: "I should always be productive" or "I should never make mistakes."
   - Impact: This creates unnecessary guilt and unrealistic standards, increasing stress and anxiety.

9. Labeling: You apply rigid, generalized definitions based on a single behavior or event.
   - Example: After forgetting an important appointment, you conclude, "I'm irresponsible."
   - Impact: This limits your ability to see the complexity of situations and people, including yourself, and can lead to hasty judgments and a rigid worldview that hinders personal growth and understanding of others.

10. Personalization: You take responsibility for external negative events.
    - Example: "My friend seems sad today. I must have done something wrong."
    - Impact: It leads to unjustified guilt and an excessive sense of responsibility.

The cumulative effect of these cognitive distortions can be significant. Often, they reinforce each other, creating a web of distorted thoughts that deeply influence your worldview. For example, a mental filter might make you focus only on the negative aspects of a situation, while overgeneralization leads you to apply this negativity to all areas of your life.

These distortions not only affect your mood but can also drive your actions in counterproductive ways. For instance, catastrophic thinking might cause you to avoid opportunities out of fear of failure, thus limiting your personal and professional growth.

Developing awareness of these distortions is essential for improving your psychological well-being. Observing your thought patterns with curiosity, rather than judgment, can help you identify which distortions frequently manifest in your life.

This self-observation process can open the door to new ways of interpreting situations, leading to more adaptive emotional and behavioral responses. With practice, you can learn to recognize these distortions in real time, creating space for more balanced and realistic perspectives.

Cognitive Schemas and Core Beliefs

Cognitive schemas are deep mental structures that shape how you interpret the world, acting like lenses through which you filter experiences, influencing your thoughts, emotions, and behaviors. Core beliefs are fundamental ideas you hold about yourself, others, and the world, often formed during childhood and adolescence. These schemas serve as mental maps, guiding how you navigate reality, shaped by significant early experiences. For example, constant criticism in childhood might lead to a schema of "inadequacy," affecting how you interpret future situations.

Core beliefs lie at the heart of these schemas, forming powerful filters like "I'm not good enough" or "The world is dangerous." These beliefs, developed through early interactions with parents, teachers, and peers, influence how you see yourself and others. Once established, schemas perpetuate themselves through confirmation bias, where you unconsciously seek out evidence that confirms your beliefs, ignoring contrary information. They also maintain themselves through behaviors that paradoxically confirm them; for example, avoiding social situations might reinforce a belief in social inadequacy.

Schemas significantly contribute to emotional and behavioral problems, such as anxiety from a "vulnerability" schema or depression from a "failure" schema. They also influence your actions, such as difficulty in forming close relationships due to a "mistrust" schema, leading to isolation and reinforcing negative beliefs. Recognizing these schemas is the first step toward change. By identifying recurring patterns in your emotional and behavioral reactions, you can begin to challenge these ingrained beliefs.

To identify core beliefs, observe the automatic thoughts that arise in stressful situations, often rooted in deeper convictions like inadequacy. Changing these schemas takes time and practice, starting by gently challenging your core beliefs and seeking evidence that contradicts them. Cognitive-behavioral therapy is particularly effective in helping you modify these dysfunctional schemas.

Schemas are learned thinking patterns, not your identity. With awareness and practice, you can change them, leading to significant improvements in your emotional well-being and quality of life. As you explore your cognitive schemas, you gain a deeper understanding of yourself and your reactions, allowing you to make more conscious choices aligned with your true values and goals.

The Impact of Dysfunctional Thoughts

Dysfunctional thoughts have a deeper impact on your daily life than you might realize. These thought patterns shape your perception of the world and unconsciously guide your actions. For instance, a single thought like "I'm not capable of this task" can trigger a chain reaction—leading you to procrastinate, which reduces the time available to complete the work. As a result, you might deliver a lower-quality outcome, reinforcing your initial belief. This self-sabotaging cycle can occur in various areas of your life, from personal relationships to your career.

In relationships, dysfunctional thoughts can create invisible barriers. You might misinterpret a friend's silence as disapproval, leading you to become defensive or distant. This behavior could actually create tension, seemingly confirming your initial interpretation. Over time, these misunderstandings can erode even the strongest relationships.

The maintenance cycle of negative thoughts often operates through a process called a "self-fulfilling prophecy." Your negative expectations influence your behavior in ways that make those expectations more likely to come true. For example, if you believe you lack social skills, you might avoid interactions, missing opportunities to improve and confirming your belief.

This cycle can also affect your work or academic performance. If you convince yourself that you're not smart enough for a task, you might put in less effort, leading to mediocre results that seem to validate your inadequacy.

However, identifying these dysfunctional thoughts brings significant benefits. It allows you to "de-center" from them, seeing them as temporary mental events rather than absolute truths, which can significantly reduce their emotional and behavioral impact.

Moreover, recognizing dysfunctional thoughts enhances your problem-solving abilities. Instead of being trapped in negative thinking patterns, you can explore alternative solutions and more constructive approaches to the challenges you face.

Another benefit is increased cognitive flexibility. As you become more adept at identifying dysfunctional thoughts, you also develop the ability to adopt multiple perspectives on a situation. This flexibility can be particularly helpful in stressful or conflictual situations, enabling you to find creative solutions to seemingly insurmountable problems.

Identifying dysfunctional thoughts can also lead to significant improvements in your emotional well-being. You might notice a reduction in symptoms of anxiety and depression as you learn to challenge the automatic negative thoughts that often fuel these moods.

In the workplace, this process can boost your productivity and satisfaction. By recognizing and challenging thoughts like "I'll never succeed," you can approach tasks with greater confidence and motivation.

The goal isn't to eliminate negative thoughts entirely, but to develop a more balanced relationship with your inner dialogue. This awareness allows you to choose how to respond to your thoughts rather than automatically reacting to them.

With practice, you may notice an improvement in your emotional resilience. Situations that once destabilized you might become more manageable as you learn to navigate your thoughts with greater skill. This increase in resilience can lead to greater emotional stability and an enhanced ability to cope with daily challenges.

Exercise 1: Automatic Thoughts Journal

For six different situations, record the event, the automatic thought you had, and the resulting emotion.

Situation	Automatic Thought	Emotion

Exercise 2: Distortion Hunt

Identify 6 recurring negative thoughts. For each one, try to pinpoint which of the 10 cognitive distortions might be at play.

Recurring Thought	Cognitive Distortion

Exercise 3: Exploring Core Beliefs

Reflect on an area of your life where you face recurring difficulties. Try to identify a possible core belief that might be at the root of these challenges.

Area of Difficulty:

_____

_____

_____

Possible Core Belief:

_____

_____

_____

Shaping Mental Health Support

Have you ever considered how your experience could positively impact someone else's life?

Imagine someone struggling with depression or anxiety, feeling lost and unsure where to turn. Your words could be the beacon of hope that guides them to the support they need. By sharing your honest thoughts about this workbook, you have the power to:

- Help someone discover effective strategies for managing their mental health challenges

- Provide insight into the practical applications of DBT, CBT, and ACT techniques

- Offer encouragement to those hesitant about taking the first step towards healing

Your perspective is unique and valuable. Whether you've found certain exercises particularly helpful, gained new insights, or even if you've encountered challenges along the way, your experience can offer invaluable guidance to others on their mental health journey.

Taking a moment to share your thoughts doesn't just help potential readers—it contributes to a broader dialogue about mental health, reducing stigma and fostering understanding. Your review, whether highlighting strengths or offering constructive feedback, plays a crucial role in refining and improving resources for those seeking help.

Remember, your honest opinion matters. Positive or critical, your feedback is equally important and appreciated. It takes just a few minutes of your time, but the impact of your words can ripple out, touching lives in ways you might never imagine.

Will you lend your voice to support others on their path to better mental health?

Thank you for being part of this important conversation.

Scan to leave a review on Amazon if you live in the US

Scan to leave a review on Amazon if you live in the UK

Scan to leave a review on Amazon if you live in Canada

Scan to leave a review on Amazon if you live in Australia

Chapter 12:

Challenging and Restructuring Thoughts

"The mind is its own place, and in itself can make a heaven of hell, a hell of heaven." -
John Milton

In this chapter, you will delve into the powerful process of cognitive restructuring. You'll learn how to identify, analyze, and modify the dysfunctional thoughts that influence your emotions and behaviors. Advanced techniques for challenging and reframing your thoughts will be explored, helping you develop a more balanced and realistic perspective on life.

Identifying, Examining, and Renewing

Transforming your thoughts begins with three key steps: identifying, examining, and renewing your ideas. Start by paying attention to the thoughts that arise, especially during intense emotions. Pause and ask yourself, "What am I thinking right now?" Write it down without judgment. A journal can be helpful.

Next, scrutinize what you've written. How accurate are these thoughts? Look for evidence both supporting and contradicting them. Consider alternative perspectives. Often, you'll find that many beliefs are based on unverified assumptions or overgeneralizations.

The next step is to create more balanced, realistic alternatives. This isn't about forced positivity but about developing a more objective view. If you've labeled yourself as "a complete failure," reframe it as "I made a mistake, but that doesn't define who I am."

This process is different from mere optimism. Rather than simply thinking, "Everything will be fine," aim for specific, realistic thoughts like, "This situation is tough, but I have the tools to handle it." Start applying this practice to mild stress situations, pausing to investigate the thoughts that precede a mood shift. Analyze them and create balanced alternatives. Gradually, apply this method to more complex challenges.

Consistency is crucial. Don't expect immediate changes; altering deeply ingrained mental habits takes time. Celebrate small victories and be patient with yourself. The impact of this mental work extends to your actions. Once you've modified a limiting thought, act accordingly. If you've reexamined your social anxiety, challenge yourself to attend an event you would have avoided. This reinforces the new thinking and triggers a positive cycle of change.

With practice, you'll get better at recognizing and challenging dysfunctional thoughts in real-time, helping you adapt to daily challenges and maintain emotional balance. The goal isn't to eliminate negative thoughts but to manage them more effectively, allowing you to take action despite their presence.

Advanced Cognitive Restructuring Techniques

To effectively address dysfunctional thoughts and develop a more balanced mindset, there are advanced techniques that can be particularly beneficial. In this section, we will explore practical strategies that enable you to challenge and reframe your thoughts, thereby enhancing your ability to manage emotions and behaviors in a more adaptive way.

The Continuum Method

The Continuum Method helps you overcome "all-or-nothing" thinking. Often, we tend to view situations in extremes, without considering the nuances in between. Imagine a line that ranges from 0 to 100. If, after making a mistake, you consider yourself a "total failure," you might initially place yourself at 0. However, upon more objective reflection, you might find that reality is closer to 40 or 50. This technique allows you to assess situations in a less drastic and more realistic manner. To apply it, identify a polarized thought, create a scale from 0 to 100, and then evaluate where you realistically stand. Consider examples of people or situations that occupy different points on the continuum to gain a more balanced perspective.

Cost-Benefit Analysis

Cost-benefit analysis is a powerful tool for evaluating the usefulness of your thought patterns. Take a recurring thought and ask yourself: "What are the advantages and disadvantages of thinking this way?" This reflection helps you see that certain thoughts, while familiar, may no longer be serving you. To use this technique, write the thought at the top of a page and divide the page into two columns: "Costs" and "Benefits." List all possible advantages and disadvantages of maintaining that thought, considering both short-term and long-term effects. Often, this analysis reveals that the costs outweigh the benefits, motivating you to seek more constructive alternatives.

The "As If" Technique

The "As If" technique invites you to act as if the alternative thought you wish to adopt is already true. This behavioral approach can be surprisingly effective in changing your beliefs. For example, if you think, "I'm too shy to make new friends," you could act as if you were a sociable person for a day. This experiment provides you with new evidence that challenges your initial belief. Choose a limiting thought you want to change, imagine how you would act if you didn't hold that belief, and plan specific actions that reflect this new way of thinking. After acting "as if," reflect on the experience and how it has influenced your initial perception.

<u>Decentering and Distancing from Thoughts</u>

Decentering and distancing techniques help you see your thoughts as temporary mental events rather than absolute truths. Instead of saying, "I'm a failure," you might say, "I'm having the thought that I'm a failure." This subtle shift creates distance between you and the thought, allowing you to observe it more objectively. To practice decentering, observe your thoughts as if they were clouds in the sky or objects on a conveyor belt. Notice them without judging or trying to change them, and consider naming your thoughts, such as "Here comes the failure thought again." These techniques help you disidentify from your thoughts, reducing their emotional power over you.

These advanced cognitive restructuring techniques work together to enhance your ability to address and manage dysfunctional thoughts. The Continuum Method challenges extreme perceptions, cost-benefit analysis evaluates the usefulness of your thoughts, the "As If" technique encourages you to act differently, and decentering offers a new perspective on your mental processes. With regular practice, you will develop greater cognitive flexibility and emotional resilience, improving your overall quality of life.

The Downward Arrow Technique

The Downward Arrow Technique is a powerful tool for delving beneath the surface of your thoughts to uncover the core beliefs that drive them. It works as an in-depth exploration of your mind, allowing you to peel back layers of thoughts until you reach the core of your beliefs.

The primary goal of this technique is to identify the fundamental beliefs that shape your thinking and behavior. Often, the thoughts that cause you distress are just the tip of the iceberg. The Downward Arrow Technique helps you uncover what lies beneath the surface.

To use this technique, start with a distressing thought and ask yourself, "If this were true, what would it mean for me?" The answer to this question becomes the starting point for the next question, and so on. Continue this process until you reach a core belief that feels fundamental and not reducible any further.

Here's a practical example:

Initial thought: "I made a mistake at work."

- "If this were true, what would it mean?"

- Answer: "It means I'm not competent at my job."

- "If you're not competent at your job, what would that mean?"

- Answer: "I could lose my job."

- "If you lost your job, what would that mean?"

- Answer: "I wouldn't be able to support myself."

- "If you couldn't support yourself, what would that mean?"

- Answer: "I would be a failure as an adult."

In this example, the core belief might be "I am a failure" or "I'm not capable of meeting others' expectations."

Another example might start from a social thought:

Initial thought: "I said something stupid during the conversation."

- "If this were true, what would it mean?"

- Answer: "People will think I'm stupid."

- "If people think you're stupid, what would that mean?"

- Answer: "No one will want to be my friend."

- "If no one wants to be your friend, what would that mean?"

- Answer: "I will be alone."

- "If you were alone, what would that mean?"

- Answer: "I am unworthy of love."

Here, the core belief could be "I am not worthy of love or acceptance."

As you use this technique, you may find that different chains of thoughts lead to the same core belief. This is a sign that you've identified a fundamental belief influencing many aspects of your life. It's important to approach this process with curiosity and self-compassion. The goal is not to judge yourself but to better understand how your mind operates. Once you've identified your core beliefs, you can begin to challenge them and develop more adaptive alternatives.

The Downward Arrow Technique can be emotionally intense, as it brings you face-to-face with deeply rooted beliefs. If you start to feel overwhelmed, take a break and remember that these beliefs, no matter how true they might seem, are just thoughts—not indisputable facts.

Reframing Thoughts

To develop a more balanced mindset, it's essential to adopt strategies that allow you to see situations from different perspectives. Instead of sticking to just one point of view, ask yourself what other interpretations might exist. When you encounter a negative thought, try exploring possible nuances or exceptions.

One effective method is to use "probability language." We often think in absolute terms, like "I will definitely fail." Reframing this thought as "It's possible I might face difficulties, but it's equally possible that I will succeed" allows you to maintain a more open and less anxious outlook on situations.

Another approach is to view situations through the eyes of a "benevolent external observer." Imagine yourself as a compassionate friend evaluating the situation from the outside. This helps you develop a less harsh judgment and reduces self-criticism.

To make these new perspectives an integral part of your thinking, it's useful to anchor them to concrete experiences. Link the new statements to specific episodes in your life where you successfully handled similar situations. This reinforces the value and credibility of the new thoughts.

Integrating these new ways of thinking into your daily routine is crucial for consolidating them. Visualization can be a valuable tool: imagine yourself acting in line with the new thoughts, thereby reinforcing their impact. Throughout the day, actively seek examples that confirm the validity of your new thoughts, and keep a journal of these instances to build a personal archive of positive experiences.

Finally, testing new thoughts through concrete actions strengthens the change. When you modify a limiting belief, act as if the new belief is already true. This will allow you to have experiences that confirm and reinforce the new way of thinking.

Reframing thoughts is an ongoing process that requires practice and patience. Over time, these new thought patterns will become automatic, helping you face daily challenges with greater resilience and optimism.

Exercise 1: Thought Court

Choose 3 recurring negative thoughts. List the evidence for and against this thought, as if you were a lawyer presenting the case in court.

Negative Thought: _____

Evidence For	Evidence Against

Negative Thought: _____

Evidence For	Evidence Against

Negative Thought: _____

Evidence For	Evidence Against

Exercise 2: Downward Arrow

Start with a disturbing thought and apply the downward arrow technique by asking yourself, "If this were true, what would it mean?" for at least 4 steps.

Initial Thought: _____

If this were true, what would it mean?

_____

_____

_____

If this were true, what would it mean?

_____

_____

_____

If this were true, what would it mean?

_____

_____

_____

If this were true, what would it mean?

_____

_____

_____

Exercise 3: Balanced Reframing

Take a negative thought you've challenged. Based on the evidence you've gathered, write a more balanced and realistic version of this thought.

Original Thought:

_____

_____

_____

Reframed Thought:

_____

_____

_____

_____

_____

_____

How do you feel with this new thought?

_____

_____

_____

_____

_____

_____

_____

Chapter 13:

CBT for Depression

"The way you think, the way you behave, the way you eat, can influence your life by 30 to 50 years." - Deepak Chopra

Depression can feel like a mental prison, but CBT offers a way out. In this chapter, you will explore how your thoughts influence your mood and how you can use cognitive and behavioral techniques to combat depression.

The Cognitive Model of Depression

Beck's cognitive triad is at the heart of the cognitive model of depression. This concept sheds light on how depression distorts your view of yourself, the world, and the future, creating a self-perpetuating cycle of negativity.

When you're depressed, you tend to see yourself in an extremely negative light. Thoughts like "I'm a failure" or "I'm worthless" become recurring. This critical view of yourself erodes your self-esteem, making you feel inadequate in many situations. Even when you achieve success, you may downplay it or attribute it to luck rather than your abilities.

The world around you takes on a bleak and threatening tone. Neutral situations are interpreted negatively, and challenges seem insurmountable. Phrases like "The world is a terrible place" or "Nothing ever goes right for me" become the lenses through which you filter your experiences. This negative perspective can lead you to withdraw from others, missing opportunities to disprove these negative beliefs.

The future appears bleak and hopeless. You expect things to go wrong and your problems to continue indefinitely. Thoughts like "Things will never get better" or "There's no way out" become constant. This pessimistic view of the future can lead to feelings of helplessness and despair, discouraging you from making plans or pursuing goals.

These depressive thoughts are not just passive reflections of your mood; they actively shape your emotions and behaviors, creating a self-sustaining cycle of depression that can feel impossible to break.

When you think "I'm a failure," you feel sad and worthless. These feelings can lead you to avoid social situations or work challenges. The resulting isolation and inactivity reinforce your belief that you're a failure, perpetuating the depressive cycle. Each avoidance becomes "proof" of your inadequacy, further fueling negative thoughts.

The maintenance cycle of depression works like this:

- Negative thoughts generate negative emotions such as sadness, anxiety, or despair.

- These negative emotions lead to avoidance behaviors or inactivity.

- Avoidance and inactivity result in a lack of positive experiences and missed opportunities to disprove negative beliefs.

- The lack of positive experiences reinforces the initial negative thoughts, closing the cycle.

For example, if you think, "I'm boring; no one wants to be with me," you may feel sad and anxious (emotion). As a result, you might decline an invitation to a party (behavior). By staying home, you miss the chance to interact positively with others and disprove your initial belief. The resulting loneliness reinforces the thought "I'm boring," perpetuating the cycle.

This cycle may seem impenetrable, but CBT offers effective tools to break it. By challenging negative thoughts and gradually changing behaviors, you can start to change your mood and perspective.

Awareness of this model is the first, crucial step toward change. Recognizing how your thoughts influence your emotions and behaviors gives you the power to intervene in the process. This doesn't mean that depression is "all in your head" or that it's your fault. Instead, it shows that there are entry points to interrupt the cycle and start feeling better.

It's important to note that the cognitive triad doesn't develop in a vacuum. Biological factors, life experiences, and chronic stress can contribute to its formation. However, once established, the triad can perpetuate depression even in the absence of the original stressors.

Typical Thoughts in Depression

When you're experiencing depression, certain negative automatic thoughts tend to recur frequently. Learning to recognize these thoughts is the first step towards challenging and overcoming them.

<u>Common Negative Thoughts:</u>

1. "I'm a failure": This thought generalizes a single mistake to your entire self-worth. It's important to remember that one mistake doesn't define who you are as a person. Try to separate what you've done from who you are.

2. "No one really cares about me": Depression often distorts your perception of relationships, making you feel isolated and unloved. However, this thought usually overlooks the people who do genuinely care about you. Take a moment to consider those positive connections, even if they seem less obvious.

3. "I'll never succeed": This negative forecast of the future can paralyze you, creating a mental barrier to change. Recognize this thought as your mind's way of trying to protect you from failure, but remind yourself of the resources and strengths you've used to overcome challenges in the past.

4. "It's all my fault": Personalization is common in depression, where you take responsibility for negative events that are often beyond your control. Try to consider the full context of a situation, thinking about other factors that may have contributed to the outcome.

5. "I'm worthless": This thought attacks your self-esteem, relying on unrealistic standards or harsh judgments. Instead, try to recognize your intrinsic value, which is not dependent on your performance or others' approval.

Strategies for Addressing Negative Thoughts:

- Develop a compassionate inner dialogue: Instead of harshly criticizing yourself, try treating yourself with the same kindness you would offer a dear friend. For example, if you make a mistake, instead of thinking "I'm an idiot," try saying, "I made a mistake, but I can learn from it."

- Create a gratitude journal: Take a few minutes each day to write down three things you're grateful for. This exercise can help balance your perspective, shifting your focus away from negative thoughts and towards what's positive in your life.

- Practice positive visualization: Imagine future scenarios where you overcome your current difficulties. This not only challenges the thought "I'll never succeed," but also helps you see the possibility of a better future, boosting motivation and optimism.

- Engage in meaningful activities: Depression often disconnects you from what once brought you joy. Rebuilding a routine that includes rewarding activities, even if they initially seem unappealing, can help break the cycle of depression. This might include creative pursuits, volunteering, or simply spending time with loved ones.

- Build a support system: Don't face depression alone. Try to connect with trusted people who can offer emotional and practical support. You might find that sharing your thoughts with someone helps you see them from a new perspective.

- Actively reframe your thoughts: Whenever you recognize a negative thought, try actively reframing it into something more balanced. If you think, "I'm a failure," reframe it to "I've made mistakes, but I can learn and improve." With repeated practice, this can gradually transform how you see yourself and your capabilities.

- Exercise and mind-body connection: Physical activity can significantly impact your mood. Even short daily walks can help you feel better both physically and mentally, breaking the cycle of negative thoughts and boosting your self-esteem.

In summary, addressing the typical thoughts of depression requires an active and mindful approach. Developing new thought and behavior patterns can be challenging, but with patience and practice, you can create a more balanced and positive perspective. This will help you navigate through the darkest moments and build a more fulfilling and meaningful life.

Behavioral Activation

Behavioral activation is a powerful technique in the fight against depression. It operates on the principle that your actions can deeply influence your thoughts and emotions. When you're depressed, there's a tendency to withdraw and avoid activities that once brought you pleasure. While this withdrawal is understandable, it also fuels the cycle of depression.

The central idea of behavioral activation is simple: act before you feel motivated. Often, when you're depressed, you wait to feel better before doing anything. However, it's the action itself that can lead to feeling better. By starting to engage in meaningful activities, even when you don't feel like it, you can break the cycle of inactivity and gradually improve your mood.

To get started, make a list of activities that you once found enjoyable or meaningful. Don't just focus on big things; include small daily activities as well. Then, schedule these activities into your routine, starting with the simplest and most accessible ones.

Techniques to Increase Your Involvement:

- Start Small: If going to the gym feels overwhelming, try taking a short walk around the block. The key is to get moving.

- Use the "5-Minute Rule": Commit to doing an activity for just five minutes. Often, once you start, you'll find it easier to continue.

- Create a Routine: Establish regular times for activities. A structured schedule can help you overcome initial resistance.

- Track Your Progress: Keep a journal of the activities you complete and how you feel afterward. This can help you see improvements over time.

- Balance Pleasure and Mastery: Include both enjoyable activities (like hobbies) and those that give you a sense of accomplishment (like completing a task).

- Be Flexible: If an activity feels too challenging on a particular day, choose a more manageable alternative.

- Involve Others: Plan activities with friends or family. Social support can boost your motivation.

- Reward Yourself: Celebrate your successes, no matter how small. Every step counts.

How Behavioral Activation Influences Mood and Thoughts:

- Breaks the Negative Cycle: Inactivity feeds negative thoughts and low self-esteem. Engaging in activities interrupts this cycle.

- Provides Evidence Against Negative Thoughts: Completing even a small task challenges the belief that you are "useless" or "incapable."

- Increases Positive Emotions: Engaging in enjoyable activities can generate positive emotions, even if they are initially mild.

- Enhances Self-Efficacy: Each time you engage in an activity despite depression, you strengthen your confidence in your ability to handle difficulties.

- Offers Healthy Distractions: Activity can temporarily distract you from negative thoughts, providing relief.

- Rebuilds Social Connections: Engaging in social activities can combat isolation, a common component of depression.

- Stimulates Physiological Changes: Physical activity, in particular, can trigger the release of endorphins and improve mood.

- Restructures Your Environment: Engaging in activities can modify your surroundings, making them more stimulating and less depressing.

It's important to remember that behavioral activation doesn't produce immediate results. At first, you might not notice a significant change in your mood. This is normal. The goal is to create positive momentum over time.

You might encounter internal resistance. Thoughts like "I don't feel like it" or "It won't make a difference" are common. Acknowledge these thoughts, but don't let them stop you. Remember, you're acting despite these thoughts, not because you feel motivated.

As you continue with behavioral activation, you may begin to notice gradual changes. You might feel a bit more energetic, or perhaps you start to experience moments of mild pleasure that weren't there before. These small changes are significant and can accumulate over time.

Behavioral activation isn't a miracle cure, but it is a powerful tool in your arsenal against depression. When combined with other CBT techniques, it can lead to significant improvements in your mood and quality of life. Remember, every step you take, no matter how small it may seem, is a step toward recovery.

Problem-Solving Techniques

Depression can make you feel overwhelmed by even the smallest problems. CBT's problem-solving approach provides a structured method for tackling challenges more effectively, reducing the sense of helplessness that often accompanies depression.

Problem-solving in CBT is based on the idea that many problems have solutions, even if they're not immediately obvious. This approach helps you break down seemingly insurmountable problems into manageable parts, allowing you to address them systematically.

<u>Steps for Effective Problem-Solving:</u>

1. Identify the Problem: Clearly define the problem. Be specific and concrete. Instead of saying, "My life is a disaster," try "I'm having trouble paying the rent this month." This specificity allows you to focus on one aspect at a time, reducing the feeling of being overwhelmed.

2. Generate Possible Solutions: Brainstorm all possible solutions without judging them. Focus on quantity over quality at this stage. Even seemingly absurd ideas can spark creative solutions. Write everything down, no matter how unlikely it seems. This process stimulates your creativity and helps you break free from habitual thought patterns.

3. Evaluate the Options: Examine the pros and cons of each solution. Consider short-term and long-term consequences. Be realistic about your current resources and abilities. This step helps you make more informed decisions and anticipate potential obstacles.

4. Choose a Solution: Select the solution that seems most practical and likely to be effective. Don't aim for the "perfect" solution, but rather the one that is "good enough." Remember, in many cases, acting imperfectly is better than not acting at all.

5. Plan the Implementation: Create a detailed action plan. Break the solution down into manageable steps. Set realistic deadlines. The more specific your plan, the more likely you are to successfully carry it out.

6. Take Action: Implement your plan. Remember, action is crucial, even if you don't feel motivated. Often, action precedes motivation, not the other way around. Start with the first step, no matter how small it may seem.

7. Review and Adapt: Assess the effectiveness of your solution. If it doesn't work as hoped, go back and try another option. This step is critical: it teaches you that failures are learning opportunities, not proof of your inadequacy.

This systematic approach to problem-solving can significantly reduce the sense of helplessness typical of depression. Here's how:

- Provides Structure: Having a clear method to follow can reduce the sense of chaos and overwhelm. Structure brings a sense of order during a time that may feel chaotic.

- Promotes Action: Instead of ruminating on problems, you focus on taking concrete steps. Action is a powerful antidote to depression.

- Increases Sense of Control: Actively addressing problems makes you feel more in control of your life. This sense of agency is crucial in combating depression.

- Challenges Negative Thoughts: Success in solving even small problems challenges the belief that you're "incompetent" or "useless." Every problem solved is evidence against these negative beliefs.

- Develops Skills: Each time you apply this process, you're improving your problem-solving skills. These skills will be valuable long after the period of depression has passed.

- Reduces Avoidance: Facing problems rather than avoiding them can reduce long-term anxiety. Avoidance provides short-term relief but feeds anxiety over time.

- Enhances Self-Efficacy: Every problem solved strengthens your confidence in handling future challenges. This confidence is a powerful antidote to depression.

Effective problem-solving takes practice. At first, it may feel difficult or artificial. Persevere. Over time, it will become more natural and automatic. It's like learning a new language: at first, it feels strange and forced, but with practice, it becomes fluent.

Start with small, manageable problems. As you gain confidence, you can tackle more complex challenges. Don't hesitate to seek support when needed. Sometimes, an outside perspective can help you see options you hadn't considered.

Finally, celebrate your successes, no matter how small they may seem. Every problem you address is a step toward overcoming depression and building greater emotional resilience. These small successes add up over time, creating a solid foundation for your future well-being.

Exercise 1: Mood and Activity Monitoring

For one week, track your mood (on a scale of 1 to 10) and the activities you engage in each day.

Date	Mood (1-10)	Activities Completed

Exercise 2: Challenging Depressive Thoughts

Identify three recurring depressive thoughts. For each one, write a more balanced response *using the CBT techniques you have learned.*

*Depressive Thought:*_____

Balanced Response:

_____

_____

*Depressive Thought:*_____

Balanced Response:

_____

_____

*Depressive Thought:*_____

Balanced Response:

_____

_____

Exercise 3: Gradual Activation Plan

List 4 activities that you once enjoyed or that you think might improve your mood. Arrange them in order of difficulty and plan when you will attempt each one.

*Activity:*_____

Action Plan:

_____

_____

*Activity:*_____

Action Plan:

_____

_____

*Activity:*_____

Action Plan:

_____

_____

*Activity:*_____

Action Plan:

_____

_____

Chapter 14:

CBT for Anxiety

"Anxiety is a thin stream of fear trickling through the mind. If encouraged, it cuts a channel into which all other thoughts are drained." - Arthur Somers Roche

Anxiety can turn your mind into a maze of worries. In this chapter, you will explore how CBT can help you navigate this maze and find calm. You'll discover how anxiety works, the different types of anxiety disorders, and effective techniques for managing it. You'll learn how to challenge anxious thoughts, reinterpret physical sensations, and gradually face feared situations.

The Cognitive Model of Anxiety

Anxiety is more than just an emotion: it's a complex system involving thoughts, physical sensations, and behaviors. These elements interact with each other, creating a cycle that can seem impossible to break.

Anxious thoughts often start with a "What if...?" "What if I fail this exam?", "What if I have a serious illness?", "What if I embarrass myself?". These thoughts trigger an immediate physical response in your body.

Your heart races, your palms sweat, your stomach tightens. These physical sensations are a natural stress response, designed to prepare you for action in dangerous situations. But with anxiety, you mistakenly interpret these signals as evidence of imminent danger.

"My heart is pounding, I must be on the verge of a heart attack," "I'm sweating so much, everyone will notice and think I'm strange." These misinterpretations further fuel anxiety, intensifying the physical sensations.

To escape this discomfort, you may engage in avoidance behaviors. You cancel the appointment, decline the invitation, postpone the task. These behaviors provide immediate relief, but in the long term, they reinforce the anxiety.

Avoidance plays a critical role in maintaining anxiety. Every time you avoid a feared situation, you miss the opportunity to challenge your fears and discover that they may not be as justified as you thought. Avoidance confirms and strengthens your belief that the situation is truly dangerous.

The anxiety cycle perpetuates itself as follows:

- An anxious thought triggers physical sensations of anxiety.

- You mistakenly interpret these sensations as signs of danger.

- This interpretation increases anxiety, intensifying the physical sensations.

- To escape this discomfort, you avoid the feared situation.

- Avoidance provides short-term relief but reinforces anxiety in the long term.

To break the anxiety cycle, CBT focuses on three key elements: thoughts, physical sensations, and behaviors. You will learn to challenge anxious thoughts, reinterpret physical sensations, and gradually face the situations you fear.

A crucial aspect of this approach is distinguishing between real and perceived dangers. Anxiety often makes us react to imagined fears as if they were real. CBT helps you assess situations more objectively, allowing you to recognize unfounded fears and reduce anxiety to manageable levels.

The goal is not to eliminate anxiety completely but to learn how to manage it so it doesn't interfere with your life. In the following sections, you'll explore specific CBT techniques for addressing different types of anxiety disorders and learn how to develop personalized strategies to manage your anxiety.

The path to overcoming anxiety may seem long and difficult, but every step you take is a step toward freedom from anxiety's grip. With practice and patience, you can learn to manage anxiety rather than let it manage you.

Types of Anxiety Disorders

<u>Generalized Anxiety Disorder (GAD)</u>

Overview:

GAD is characterized by excessive and uncontrollable worry about various aspects of daily life. This worry is persistent and often disproportionate to the actual circumstances. Individuals with GAD may find it difficult to control their worry, leading to significant distress and impairment in daily functioning.

Key Symptoms:

- Constant Worry: Persistent worry that is difficult to control, often about everyday matters such as work, finances, health, or relationships.

- Difficulty Concentrating: Trouble focusing or maintaining attention, often because the mind is preoccupied with worry.

- Restlessness: A feeling of being on edge, often accompanied by physical symptoms like fidgeting or an inability to relax.

- Muscle Tension: Chronic physical tension, particularly in the shoulders, neck, or back, which can lead to headaches or other physical complaints.

- Sleep Disturbances: Difficulty falling asleep, staying asleep, or experiencing restful sleep due to racing thoughts or anxiety.

How It Manifests:

You may find yourself constantly ruminating about work, finances, health, or relationships, even when there are no concrete reasons for concern. The worry can be about a variety of topics or specific concerns that shift from one day to the next. This chronic worry often leads to a sense of impending doom or an unrealistic fear of disaster.

CBT Strategies:

- Cognitive Restructuring: Identify and challenge cognitive distortions that contribute to your anxiety, such as catastrophizing or overgeneralization. For each distorted thought, practice generating a more balanced and evidence-based perspective.

- Mindfulness-Based Stress Reduction (MBSR): Integrate mindfulness techniques that encourage living in the present moment rather than focusing on potential future catastrophes. This approach can be particularly effective in reducing the chronic worry associated with GAD.

- Behavioral Experiments: Test your beliefs by engaging in behavioral experiments. For example, if you worry excessively about making mistakes at work, intentionally allow yourself to make a small mistake and observe the outcome. This can help you challenge the belief that every mistake leads to disaster.

- Progressive Exposure to Uncertainty: Gradually expose yourself to situations that evoke uncertainty without engaging in your usual worry behaviors. This exposure helps you build tolerance to uncertainty, a common trigger for GAD.

- Worry Time Scheduling: Set aside 15-20 minutes each day for "worry time." During this period, allow yourself to focus on your worries, but once the time is up, redirect your attention to other activities.

- Relaxation Techniques: Incorporate relaxation practices such as deep breathing exercises, progressive muscle relaxation, or mindfulness meditation into your daily routine. These techniques can help reduce the physical symptoms of anxiety and promote a sense of calm.

Case Example:

Imagine a scenario where you are constantly worried about your job security. Despite consistent positive feedback from your supervisor, you fear losing your job at any moment. Through CBT, you might explore the evidence for and against this worry, practice tolerating uncertainty by not seeking constant reassurance, and gradually shift your focus to tasks and activities that you can control.

CBT-Oriented Questions:

- What are the underlying fears driving my worry, and how realistic are they when I examine them closely?

- How would my life be different if I could reduce my worry by even 10%? What steps can I take today to move toward that change?

- What personal strengths have I overlooked that could help me manage these worries more effectively?

- If I were to observe someone else worrying in the same way, what advice would I give them?

- What does my worry protect me from, and is that protection worth the cost it has on my well-being?

Panic Disorder

Overview:

Panic Disorder is characterized by sudden and intense episodes of fear or discomfort, known as panic attacks. These attacks can occur unexpectedly and are often accompanied by physical symptoms that may feel overwhelming or life-threatening. The fear of having future attacks can lead to significant changes in behavior, such as avoiding certain places or situations.

Key Symptoms:

- Palpitations: A racing or pounding heart, often accompanied by a feeling of being out of control.

- Sweating: Excessive sweating, even in the absence of physical exertion or heat.

- Trembling: Shaking or trembling, sometimes so severe that it is visibly noticeable.

- Shortness of Breath: A feeling of being unable to breathe or suffocating, which can trigger further panic.

- Fear of Losing Control or Dying: A profound fear that the panic attack might lead to death or that you might lose control of yourself.

How It Manifests: You may experience sudden, intense panic attacks that seem to come out of nowhere. These attacks are often accompanied by a fear of dying, losing control, or going crazy. The unpredictability of these attacks can lead to a persistent fear of having another one, causing you to avoid situations or places where you think an attack might occur.

CBT Strategies:

- Interoceptive Exposure: Deliberately trigger the physical sensations associated with panic attacks (such as dizziness or shortness of breath) in a controlled setting. This helps you learn that these sensations, while uncomfortable, are not dangerous.

- Breathing Techniques: Practice slow, deep breathing exercises to help regulate your breathing and reduce hyperventilation during a panic attack.

- Cognitive Restructuring: Challenge catastrophic thoughts about panic attacks, such as the belief that you might die or lose control. Replace these thoughts with more realistic and calming statements.

- Behavioral Experiments: Gradually expose yourself to situations you avoid due to fear of panic attacks. Start with less intimidating scenarios and work your way up to more challenging ones.

- Grounding Techniques: Use grounding strategies, such as focusing on the sensations of an object in your hand or the feeling of your feet on the ground, to stay connected to the present moment during a panic attack.

Case Example:

Imagine that you experience a panic attack while driving, leading you to avoid driving altogether. Through CBT, you might work on interoceptive exposure by simulating the physical sensations of panic in a safe environment. You could then gradually reintroduce driving, starting with short trips around your neighborhood and progressively increasing the distance as your confidence grows.

CBT-Oriented Questions:

- What evidence do I have that my worst fears during a panic attack will actually come true?

- How have I coped with panic attacks in the past, and what strategies have helped me manage them?"

- What would happen if I allowed myself to fully experience the sensations of panic without trying to escape or avoid them?

- How might avoiding situations due to fear of panic attacks be limiting my life, and what small steps could I take to reclaim those areas?

- What can I learn from my panic attacks about the thoughts and beliefs that fuel my anxiety?

Specific Phobias

Overview:

Specific Phobias are intense, irrational fears of particular objects or situations, such as heights, flying, spiders, or enclosed spaces. These fears are typically out of proportion to the actual danger posed by the object or situation and can lead to significant distress or avoidance behaviors.

Key Symptoms:

- Intense Fear: An overwhelming sense of fear or panic when confronted with the phobic stimulus.

- Avoidance Behavior: Actively avoiding the feared object or situation, which can interfere with daily life.

- Physical Symptoms: Rapid heartbeat, sweating, trembling, or shortness of breath when exposed to the phobic stimulus.

- Anticipatory Anxiety: Worrying about encountering the phobic stimulus even when it is not present.

How It Manifests:

You may experience a strong, uncontrollable fear when faced with a specific object or situation, such as being in a small elevator, seeing a snake, or flying on an airplane. This fear can be so intense that you go to great lengths to avoid the object or situation, which can limit your activities and reduce your quality of life.

CBT Strategies:

- Exposure Therapy: Gradually expose yourself to the feared object or situation in a controlled and systematic way. Start with less frightening scenarios and slowly work your way up to the more challenging ones.

- Cognitive Restructuring: Identify and challenge the irrational beliefs that fuel your phobia. Replace catastrophic thoughts with more balanced and realistic ones.

- Relaxation Techniques: Use deep breathing, progressive muscle relaxation, or mindfulness to manage anxiety during exposure exercises.

- Visualization: Before confronting your phobia in real life, practice visualizing yourself successfully managing the situation. This can help build confidence and reduce fear.

- Graded Exposure: Create a fear hierarchy, ranking situations from least to most frightening, and tackle them one at a time.

Case Example:

If you have a fear of flying, you might start by looking at pictures of airplanes, then watching videos of flights, followed by visiting an airport, and eventually taking a short flight. Throughout this process, you would use relaxation techniques and cognitive restructuring to manage your anxiety and build confidence.

CBT-Oriented Questions:

- What is the worst thing that could realistically happen if I confront my phobia, and how likely is that outcome

- How does avoiding my phobia impact my life and what might I gain if I were able to face it

- What evidence do I have that my fear is as dangerous as I perceive it to be

- In what small ways can I begin to expose myself to the object or situation I fear

- How would my life change if I could reduce or eliminate my phobia

Social Anxiety Disorder (SAD)

Overview:

Social Anxiety Disorder, also known as Social Phobia, involves an overwhelming fear of social situations where you may be scrutinized or judged. This fear can lead to significant avoidance of social interactions, impacting various aspects of life.

Key Symptoms:

- Fear of Judgment: Persistent worry about being negatively evaluated in social settings.

- Avoidance Behavior: Steering clear of social events, conversations, or public performances to escape potential embarrassment.

- Physical Symptoms: Experiencing symptoms like blushing, sweating, or trembling when faced with social situations.

- Anticipatory Anxiety: Intense anxiety that builds up days or even weeks before a social event.

How It Manifests:

You may find yourself frequently declining invitations to social gatherings or avoiding situations where you need to interact with others, fearing that you might say or do something embarrassing. This avoidance can lead to missed opportunities and a growing sense of isolation.

CBT Strategies:

- Imaginal Exposure: Visualize and mentally rehearse social situations that provoke anxiety. By repeatedly imagining these scenarios and the potential outcomes, you can reduce your fear response when encountering them in real life.

- Self-Compassion Practice: Develop self-compassion techniques to counteract harsh self-criticism. This might include writing compassionate letters to yourself or using self-affirming language when you notice self-critical thoughts.

- Decatastrophizing: Engage in exercises that help you break down the worst-case scenarios you fear in social situations. Challenge these catastrophic thoughts by assessing their likelihood and considering more realistic outcomes.

- Behavioral Activation: Identify and engage in social activities that align with your values and interests, gradually increasing the frequency and complexity of these activities to build confidence.

- Video Feedback: Record yourself during a social interaction (with permission), and then review the footage to identify discrepancies between your perception of how you performed and the reality. This can help you recognize and challenge distorted beliefs about how you come across to others.

Case Example:

Suppose you fear attending networking events because you believe you'll say something foolish. You might start by practicing small talk in low-stakes environments, like with a barista or a coworker. Over time, you could work up to attending a small networking event, using imaginal exposure to rehearse positive interactions beforehand.

CBT-Oriented Questions:

- What specific evidence do I have that others are judging me as critically as I fear?

- How might I be underestimating my ability to handle social situations effectively?

- In what ways could my avoidance of social interactions be perpetuating my anxiety?

- How can I practice self-compassion when I feel anxious in social settings?

- What are some steps I can take to challenge my beliefs about social failure and build confidence in my interactions?

Obsessive-Compulsive Disorder (OCD)

Overview:

Obsessive-Compulsive Disorder (OCD) is characterized by intrusive, unwanted thoughts (obsessions) and repetitive behaviors or mental acts (compulsions) that the individual feels driven to perform to reduce the anxiety caused by these obsessions.

Key Symptoms:

- Intrusive Thoughts: Recurrent and persistent thoughts, images, or impulses that are intrusive and cause significant anxiety.

- Compulsive Behaviors: Repetitive behaviors (e.g., handwashing, checking) or mental acts (e.g., counting, repeating words) that are performed to neutralize the obsessions or prevent a feared event.

- Distress and Interference: The obsessions and compulsions are time-consuming and cause significant distress or impairment in daily functioning.

- Recognition: Most individuals with OCD recognize that their obsessions or compulsions are excessive or irrational, but they feel unable to stop them.

How It Manifests:

You might find yourself repeatedly checking if doors are locked, washing your hands until they are sore, or mentally reviewing your actions to ensure you haven't harmed someone. These behaviors or mental acts are performed in an attempt to relieve the distress caused by obsessive thoughts, but they only provide temporary relief, leading to a cycle of anxiety and compulsion.

CBT Strategies:

- Exposure and Response Prevention (ERP): Gradually expose yourself to the thoughts, images, or situations that trigger your obsessions without engaging in the compulsive behaviors that usually follow. Over time, this helps reduce the anxiety associated with the obsessions and weakens the compulsion.

- Cognitive Restructuring: Identify and challenge the catastrophic thoughts that drive your compulsions. For instance, if you fear contamination, examine the evidence for and against the likelihood of becoming seriously ill from touching a doorknob.

- Thought Stopping Techniques: Use techniques to interrupt obsessive thoughts, such as visualizing a stop sign or saying "Stop!" out loud or in your mind when you notice a repetitive thought starting to take hold.

- Mindfulness-Based Cognitive Therapy (MBCT): Incorporate mindfulness practices to help you observe your thoughts without judgment, reducing the power they have over you and preventing you from getting caught up in the compulsion cycle.

- Behavioral Experiments: Design experiments to test the validity of your obsessive thoughts. For example, if you fear leaving the stove on, deliberately leave it off and resist the urge to check it repeatedly. Record the outcome and your emotional response to reinforce that the compulsion is unnecessary.

Case Example:

Imagine you are constantly checking whether you've locked your front door because you fear a break-in. Using ERP, you might start by locking the door once and walking away without checking it again, even though this causes significant anxiety. Over time, and with repeated practice, the urge to check decreases, and you begin to feel more in control of your thoughts and actions.

CBT-Oriented Questions:

- What is the evidence that something bad will happen if I don't perform my compulsion?

- How can I gradually reduce the frequency or intensity of my compulsive behaviors?

- What are the long-term costs of engaging in my compulsions, and how might I benefit from resisting them?

- How do my compulsions reinforce the power of my obsessive thoughts?

- What would it feel like to sit with the discomfort of not performing a compulsion, and how might I learn from this experience?

Post-Traumatic Stress Disorder (PTSD)

Overview:

Post-Traumatic Stress Disorder (PTSD) can develop after experiencing or witnessing a traumatic event. It involves persistent, distressing symptoms that interfere with daily life, including reliving the trauma, avoiding reminders of the event, and experiencing heightened emotional arousal.

Key Symptoms:

- Intrusive Memories: Recurrent, involuntary, and distressing memories of the traumatic event, including flashbacks where the person feels as though they are reliving the trauma.

- Avoidance: Efforts to avoid thoughts, feelings, conversations, activities, places, or people that remind the individual of the traumatic event.

- Negative Mood and Cognitions: Persistent negative emotional states, distorted blame of oneself or others, diminished interest in activities, and feelings of detachment from others.

- Hyperarousal: Increased arousal and reactivity, including being easily startled, having difficulty sleeping, experiencing irritability or anger outbursts, and having trouble concentrating.

How It Manifests:

You might find yourself reliving the trauma through flashbacks or nightmares, avoiding places or situations that remind you of the event, and feeling constantly on edge. These symptoms can lead to significant distress and make it difficult to function in everyday life, impacting relationships, work, and overall well-being.

CBT Strategies:

- Trauma-Focused CBT: Engage in therapy that specifically addresses the trauma, working through the memories of the event in a safe and structured way to reduce their emotional power over you.

- Exposure Therapy: Gradually confront the memories, situations, and feelings associated with the trauma in a controlled and safe environment. This can help decrease the fear and distress they provoke over time.

- Cognitive Processing Therapy (CPT): Identify and challenge unhelpful thoughts related to the trauma, such as self-blame or guilt, and replace them with more balanced and compassionate perspectives.

- Relaxation Techniques: Practice relaxation exercises, such as deep breathing, progressive muscle relaxation, or guided imagery, to manage hyperarousal and reduce the physiological symptoms of PTSD.

- Grounding Techniques: Use grounding strategies to stay connected to the present moment during flashbacks or periods of intense distress. This might include focusing on your breathing, describing your surroundings in detail, or using physical sensations (e.g., holding a cold object) to anchor yourself in reality.

Case Example:

Imagine that after a car accident, you experience flashbacks whenever you drive or even think about getting into a car. Through CBT, you might work on gradually exposing yourself to the act of driving, starting with sitting in a parked car and progressing to short drives. Concurrently, you might address any self-blame or fear of losing control, learning to reframe these thoughts more positively and realistically.

CBT-Oriented Questions:

- How does avoiding reminders of the trauma impact my ability to heal and move forward?

- What evidence do I have that challenges the negative beliefs I hold about myself or the world since the trauma?

- How can I gradually reintroduce myself to situations I've been avoiding because of the trauma?

- What are the physical sensations I experience during flashbacks, and how can I use grounding techniques to manage them?

- How might revisiting the trauma in a controlled and safe environment help me reduce its emotional impact?

The Anxiety Cycle

The anxiety cycle is a process where thoughts, emotions, and behaviors interact, intensifying and perpetuating anxiety. Understanding this cycle is crucial for effectively breaking it.

Anatomy of the Cycle:

- Trigger: The cycle begins with a triggering event, which can be either external (a situation) or internal (a thought or physical sensation).

- Interpretation: Immediately after the trigger, you interpret it. If you are prone to anxiety, you're likely to interpret the event as a threat.

- Anxious Thoughts: This interpretation generates anxious thoughts like "What if the worst happens?" or "I can't handle this."

- Physical Reaction: Your body responds to these thoughts by activating the "fight or flight" response. Your heart rate increases, muscles tense, and breathing becomes shallow.

- Emotions: These physical sensations fuel feelings of fear and anxiety.

- Behaviors: To alleviate this discomfort, you may engage in avoidance or safety behaviors.

- Reinforcement: These behaviors offer short-term relief but ultimately reinforce anxiety, increasing sensitivity to future triggers.

Example:

- Trigger: You need to speak in public.

- Interpretation: "This is going to be a disaster."

- Thoughts: "I'll make a fool of myself. Everyone will judge me."

- Physical Reaction: Sweating, trembling, nausea.

- Emotions: Intense anxiety and fear.

- Behaviors: You avoid the task or rely on safety strategies like reading verbatim from notes.

- Reinforcement: Avoidance confirms your fear, making future similar situations even harder to face.

Points of Intervention:

- Interpreting the Trigger: Challenge the initial threat interpretation.

- Anxious Thoughts: Identify and reframe catastrophic thinking.

- Physical Reaction: Use relaxation techniques to calm the physical response.

- Emotions: Practice tolerating anxious emotions without immediately reacting.

- Behaviors: Resist the urge to avoid, and gradually face feared situations.

Strategies to Break the Cycle:

- Cognitive Restructuring: Identify automatic anxious thoughts and challenge them with questions like "What evidence do I have that this thought is true?" Develop more realistic interpretations.

- Relaxation Techniques: Practice diaphragmatic breathing or progressive muscle relaxation to calm your body's physical response to anxiety.

- Mindfulness: Observe your thoughts and sensations without judgment. Stay grounded in the present moment rather than getting lost in worry.

- Gradual Exposure: Create a hierarchy of feared situations and gradually expose yourself to them, starting with the least anxiety-provoking. Stay in the situation until the anxiety naturally decreases.

- Behavioral Experiments: Test your anxious predictions with small experiments. Collect objective evidence about the validity of your fears.

- Modifying Safety Behaviors: Identify the behaviors you use to feel "safe" (e.g., avoiding eye contact) and gradually reduce them, proving to yourself that you can manage without them.

- Acceptance and Tolerance of Anxiety: Recognize that a certain level of anxiety is normal and acceptable. Practice being willing to feel anxious without immediately trying to eliminate it.

- Reframing Anxiety: Interpret anxiety as excitement or energy. Use phrases like "I'm excited about this challenge" instead of "I'm anxious."

- External Focus: Shift your attention from yourself to your surroundings or the task at hand. Focus on what you are doing rather than how you feel.

- Self-Compassion: Treat yourself with kindness when you feel anxious. Remember that anxiety is a common human experience.

Practical Application:

When you notice the anxiety cycle beginning, pause and apply a grounding technique:

Anchoring Technique: Focus on the physical sensations in your body. Feel your feet on the ground, notice your breathing, and bring your attention to something tangible in your environment. This can help you stay present and reduce the escalation of anxiety.

Gradual Exposure

Gradual exposure is one of the most effective techniques in CBT for managing anxiety. It's based on the idea that by gradually facing the situations that cause anxiety, rather than avoiding them, you can reduce fear and change how your brain responds to these triggers. When you avoid a feared situation, you might feel temporary relief, but in the long run, this avoidance reinforces your anxiety. Gradual exposure helps break this cycle.

To start, it's essential to create an exposure hierarchy. This hierarchy is a list of situations that trigger your anxiety, ranked from least to most frightening. For example, if you're afraid of public speaking, your hierarchy might start with speaking in front of a mirror, then progress to speaking in front of a friend, and eventually lead to giving a presentation in front of a group. The goal is to gradually face these situations, starting with those that cause a manageable level of anxiety.

When creating your hierarchy, be specific. Instead of listing something general like "public speaking," break the activity down into smaller, concrete steps. Assign each situation an anxiety score from 0 to 100, based on how scary you find it. This will help you identify which situation to tackle first and which to save for later when you feel more confident.

During exposure, it's normal to experience an increase in anxiety. This is expected. The goal isn't to avoid these feelings but to learn how to manage them. Techniques like deep breathing can help you stay calm. Inhale slowly and deeply through your nose, hold your breath for a few seconds, and then exhale slowly through your mouth to reduce physical tension. These techniques can help you stay in the situation long enough for the anxiety to naturally subside.

Another useful approach is positive self-talk. Instead of getting overwhelmed by negative thoughts like "I can't do this," try repeating reassuring phrases to yourself like "I'm learning to handle this" or "This discomfort will pass." These positive messages can help shift your perspective and reduce the anxiety you feel.

The key to effective exposure is gradual progress and repetition. You don't need to conquer the most difficult situation right away. Tackle each step calmly, repeating the exposure until you notice a significant reduction in anxiety. Only then should you move on to the next level in your hierarchy. This method allows you to build confidence and train your brain to respond differently to anxiety-provoking stimuli.

It's also important to maintain some flexibility in the process. If a step proves too challenging, take a step back and repeat a previous step until you feel ready to move forward. There's no rush. The goal is progress, not perfection.

Gradual exposure is not an easy path, but it is one of the most effective ways to overcome anxiety. Every small victory brings you closer to a life less dominated by fear. CBT provides you with the tools to face your anxieties and take control of your life, one step at a time.

Exercise 1: Anxiety Diary

For 4 episodes of anxiety, record the situation, anxious thoughts, physical sensations, and resulting behaviors.

Situation	Anxious Thoughts	Physical Sensations	Resulting Behaviors

Exercise 2: Reinterpreting Physical Sensations

List 4 physical sensations you associate with anxiety. For each, write down an anxious interpretation and then provide a more realistic alternative explanation.

Physical Sensation	Anxious Interpretation	Alternative Explanation

Exercise 3: Exposure Hierarchy

Identify a situation you avoid due to anxiety. Create an exposure hierarchy with five steps, ranging from least to most anxiety-provoking.

Situation to Address:

_____

Exposure Steps:

Step 1: Description of the least anxiety-provoking action.

_____

_____

Step 2: Description of a slightly more anxiety-provoking action.

_____

_____

Step 3: Description of a moderately anxiety-provoking action.

_____

_____

Step 4: Description of a highly anxiety-provoking action.

_____

_____

Step 5: Description of the most anxiety-provoking action.

_____

_____

Chapter 15:

CBT for Anger Management

"Anger is an acid that can do more harm to the vessel in which it is stored than to anything on which it is poured." - Mark Twain

Anger is an intense emotional response to perceived threats, injustice, or frustration. It manifests through physiological changes such as increased heart rate and blood pressure, often accompanied by hostile thoughts and aggressive behaviors. This chapter explores how Cognitive Behavioral Therapy (CBT) provides tools to understand and manage anger effectively.

Understanding Anger

Anger arises from a complex cognitive process influenced by automatic thoughts and deep-seated beliefs. These thoughts, often unconscious, quickly interpret situations based on past experiences and personal beliefs. For instance, if a colleague criticizes your work, you might automatically think, "They're trying to discredit me," or "I'm never good enough." These interpretations, rather than the event itself, trigger the emotional response of anger.

Deep-seated beliefs, such as "I must always be perfect" or "Others should never criticize me," act as lenses through which you filter experiences. These beliefs can amplify the perception of threat or injustice, further fueling your anger.

The cycle of anger develops through distinct stages:

1. Trigger: An external event (like criticism) or internal event (such as an unpleasant memory) initiates the process.

2. Interpretation: You quickly evaluate the situation, often in a distorted way. A common interpretation might be, "They are attacking me personally."

3. Physical Activation: The body prepares for action. Your heart rate increases, muscles tense up, and your breathing becomes rapid.

4. Emotional Intensification: Anger builds, often accompanied by other emotions such as frustration or fear.

5. Reactive Behavior: You act impulsively out of anger. This might involve raising your voice, using aggressive language, or even resorting to physical violence.

6. Consequences: Your actions affect the situation and your relationships, often negatively.

7. Reflection: After the anger subsides, you may feel guilt or regret for your behavior.

Recognizing the early signs of anger is crucial for intervening before the emotion spirals out of control. These signs vary from person to person but generally include:

Physical Signs:

- Muscle tension, especially in the jaw or hands
- Increased heart rate
- Feeling of warmth or redness in the face
- Rapid or shallow breathing

Emotional Signs:

- Growing irritability
- A sense of internal pressure or "boiling"
- Difficulty concentrating

Cognitive Signs:

- Thoughts of revenge or retaliation
- "Tunnel vision," focusing only on the negative aspects of the situation
- Difficulty considering alternative perspectives

To break the cycle of anger, you can intervene at various stages:

During the Interpretation Stage: Challenge your automatic evaluations. Ask yourself, "Are there other possible explanations for this behavior?" or "Am I jumping to conclusions?" This can help you consider alternative perspectives and reduce the intensity of your emotional response.

During Physical Activation: Use relaxation techniques to calm your body. Diaphragmatic breathing is particularly effective: breathe deeply through your nose, counting to 4, hold the breath for 4 seconds, then exhale slowly through your mouth, counting to 6. Repeat this cycle several times.

During Emotional Intensification: Practice emotional awareness. Acknowledge the anger without judgment, observing it as a wave that rises and falls. You can give it a name: "Here comes the anger." This approach can create psychological distance from the emotion, making it more manageable.

Before Reactive Behavior: Take a pause. Count to 10 or temporarily remove yourself from the situation if possible. Use this time to reflect on the potential consequences of your actions and consider more constructive responses.

During the Reflection Stage: Analyze the anger episode. Identify the triggers, automatic thoughts, and behaviors that contributed to the escalation. This analysis will help you develop strategies for managing similar situations in the future.

Learning to recognize and intervene in the different stages of the anger cycle requires practice and patience. Over time, you will develop greater awareness of your thought patterns and reactions, allowing you to manage anger more effectively and constructively.

Relational Anger

Effectively managing anger requires a deep emotional awareness. Recognizing your emotions as they begin to surface is crucial in preventing anger from escalating. Emotional awareness allows you to identify the early signs of anger, such as growing frustration or the feeling of being overwhelmed, before these emotions lead to harmful actions. This level of self-awareness gives you the opportunity to intervene early, choosing a more balanced and constructive response.

When you start to feel anger rising, it's helpful to take a pause and communicate your emotional state to the other person clearly and non-aggressively. Nonviolent Communication (NVC) is a powerful tool for expressing your feelings without blaming the other person. An effective NVC format might be: "When [specific situation], I feel [emotion] because I need [unmet need]. I would prefer [specific request]." For example, instead of saying, "You always make me angry when you ignore what I say," you could rephrase it as, "When I feel like my opinions aren't being heard, I feel frustrated because I need to feel respected. I would prefer that we take some time to discuss our views."

Using this language reduces the likelihood of triggering a defensive reaction in the other person, opening the door to a more constructive dialogue. Additionally, by using NVC, you set an example of how to handle conflicts in a healthier and more respectful way, which can significantly improve the quality of communication within the relationship.

Empathy also plays a crucial role in managing anger within relationships. Cultivating empathy means making an effort to understand the emotions and perspectives of the other person. A practical technique for developing empathy is reflective listening. After the other person has spoken, you repeat what you heard in your own words to ensure understanding. For example, "So, if I understand correctly, you felt neglected when I didn't respond to your message right away." This type of response not only shows that you are actively listening, but it can also help defuse tension by showing the other person that their feelings are valid and understood.

Post-conflict repair work is essential for maintaining a healthy relationship. It's not enough to simply apologize; repair requires concrete actions to rebuild trust. After an episode of anger, taking the time for a "post-conflict check-in" can be extremely beneficial. This dedicated moment allows both parties to share how they felt during the conflict, discuss what worked and what could be improved in the future. For instance, you might agree on new ways to communicate during tense situations, such as taking a break before continuing a difficult discussion. This practice not only helps heal emotional wounds but also strengthens the relationship by demonstrating a mutual commitment to growth and understanding.

A key aspect of post-conflict repair is understanding that every episode of anger offers an opportunity for reflection and improvement. It's not just about resolving the specific incident but learning from past experiences to prevent future conflicts. For example, after repairing the damage caused by a heated argument, you might ask yourself, "What can I do differently next time?" and "How can I manage my emotions better?" Repair work is an essential part of maintaining a healthy and resilient relationship.

Beyond repair, it's important to dedicate time to self-reflection. Reflective questions can help you examine your thought and behavior patterns within the relationship. For example, you might ask yourself, "In what situations do I tend to react with anger? What triggers me?" Analyzing the triggers and underlying beliefs that fuel your anger can help you identify areas for improvement. For instance, you may discover that your anger often stems from feeling ignored or disrespected. Recognizing this belief allows you to explore it more deeply and ask yourself, "How can I modify this belief? Is it really true that every time someone doesn't listen to me, they are intentionally being disrespectful?"

Awareness of these dynamics enables you to approach situations more rationally and less emotionally. For example, if you identify that your aggressive reaction is rooted in a fear of abandonment, you can work on strategies to emotionally reassure yourself without resorting to anger. This awareness makes you more responsible for your reactions, allowing you to choose responses that are more mindful and less impulsive.

To delve even deeper, explore your emotional needs in relation to others. Often, anger is a response to the frustration of unmet needs. For example, you might have a deep need for respect or to feel heard and valued. When these needs are not met, anger can easily surface as a defense mechanism. Asking yourself, "What are my unmet needs in this situation?" can offer you a different and less reactive perspective. Additionally, it's helpful to communicate these needs openly and in a non-confrontational way: instead of using anger to express them, you can verbalize them directly, facilitating a more empathetic response from the other person.

Another useful technique is to engage in specific reparative actions. If, for example, you raised your voice or said something hurtful during a conflict, you could suggest doing something concrete to repair the damage. This might be a simple gesture like writing an apology note, offering quality time, or making an effort to show that you are actively working on improving the behavior that caused the conflict. Concrete repair strengthens trust and demonstrates to the other person that you are committed to improvement.

Cultivating empathy is not only useful during conflicts but can also be preventive. If you regularly make an effort to put yourself in the other person's shoes and understand their perspectives and feelings, it's less likely that anger will reach intense levels. You can ask yourself, "How does the other person feel in this situation? What could I do to ease the tension and improve communication?" This approach helps you maintain a more balanced perspective and encourages you to respond with more kindness and understanding.

Consistently using these strategies in relationships can help you not only reduce the frequency and intensity of conflicts but also create an environment of mutual trust and respect. Relationships improve not because conflicts disappear, but because conflicts are addressed constructively and with a willingness to grow together.

Thought Patterns That Fuel Anger

Anger often stems from specific thought patterns that distort your perception of situations and amplify your emotional reactions. These patterns, rooted in deep-seated beliefs and distorted interpretations, can turn even minor events into causes of intense anger. Here are some of the key thought patterns that fuel anger:

- Revenge Thinking: When you're angry, you might find yourself fantasizing about getting back at someone or making them pay for the wrong they did to you. This type of thinking gives you an illusion of control and justice, but in reality, it only intensifies and prolongs your anger, making it harder to resolve the issue constructively.

- Injustice Thinking: This pattern is based on the belief that something profoundly wrong or unfair has been done to you. You might think, "This shouldn't be happening" or "This is unacceptable." Such thoughts feed a sense of indignation and resentment, causing you to fixate on the perceived injustice rather than seeking solutions.

- Catastrophic Anger Thinking: In this case, you perceive the consequences of a situation as disastrous and irreparable. You might think, "This will ruin everything" or "I'll never recover from this." This kind of thinking amplifies your emotional reaction, making you feel powerless and trapped, and often leads to impulsive behaviors that worsen the situation.

- Personalization Thinking: Here, you interpret others' actions as personal attacks against you, even when they are not. For example, if someone interrupts you during a conversation, you might think, "They're intentionally disrespecting me" or "They think I'm not smart enough." This type of thinking not only fuels your anger but can also damage long-term relationships.

- Should Thinking: This pattern is based on rigid beliefs about how others should behave or how things should go. You might think, "They should treat me with more respect" or "Things should always go my way." When these expectations aren't met, anger can easily arise, fueled by frustration.

- Overestimation of Danger Thinking: This pattern leads you to perceive situations as more threatening than they actually are. You might think, "If I don't react immediately, things will get worse" or "I have to defend myself right now." Such thinking can cause you to overreact, fueling anger and creating further conflict.

- Judgmental Thinking: In this case, you are prone to harshly judging others or yourself. You might think, "That person is terrible" or "I'm an idiot for letting this happen." These thoughts not only fuel your anger but also often lead to a distorted and negative view of people and situations.

- Disqualification of the Positive Thinking: In this case, you tend to ignore or minimize any positive aspects of the situation or others' actions, focusing solely on what you consider negative. You might think, "Even if they apologized, it means nothing" or "They did one thing right, but that doesn't erase all the wrongs." This type of thinking prevents you from seeing the positive sides of situations, further fueling your anger.

- Overgeneralization Thinking: Here, you take a single event or behavior and extend it into a global generalization. You might think, "Everyone is against me" or "Things always go wrong for me." This thought pattern amplifies your frustration and anger, making you feel helpless and in a hopeless situation.

- Polarized Thinking: This pattern views situations in extreme terms, with no room for nuance or middle ground. You might think, "Either you do exactly what I say, or you don't care about me at all" or "If I don't win, I'm a total loser." This type of thinking fuels anger and resentment, leading you to interpret situations in a rigid and inflexible way.

- External Blame Thinking: This pattern leads you to constantly blame others for your problems or discomfort. You might think, "It's all their fault that I feel this way" or "If it weren't for them, I wouldn't have these issues." This thinking prevents you from seeing your role in situations, fueling anger towards others and creating a cycle of resentment.

- Magnification of Offenses Thinking: Here, you excessively magnify the importance of perceived offenses. You might think, "I can't believe they said/did that, it's unforgivable" or "This is the worst thing that could have happened to me." This type of thinking intensifies your anger and leads you to react disproportionately to the actual offense.

- Self-Fulfilling Prophecy Thinking: In this case, you convince yourself that your negative predictions about how things will go are inevitable, leading you to behave in a way that makes your expectations come true. You might think, "I know this argument will end badly, so I might as well react now" or "There's no way to resolve this, so why bother trying?" This thinking not only fuels your anger but often contributes to creating the negative outcome you feared.

- Rumination Thinking: This pattern leads you to repeatedly replay an event or offense in your mind, keeping your anger alive long after the event has occurred. You might think, "I can't stop thinking about what they said/did" or "Every time I think about it, I get angry again." This thinking fuels your anger over time and makes it harder to let go of resentment.

- Justification of Anger Thinking: In this case, you convince yourself that your anger is always justified and legitimate, regardless of the situation. You might think, "I have every right to be angry" or "If I don't get angry, it means I'm weak." This type of thinking makes it difficult to objectively evaluate your anger and consider more constructive responses.

These thought patterns distort your interpretation of events, making it difficult to respond in a balanced and constructive manner. Identifying them is the first step toward learning how to manage anger more effectively.

Once you've identified the thought patterns that fuel your anger, it's essential to apply effective strategies to modify and manage them. Here are some techniques that can help you respond in a more balanced and constructive way:

- Anger Thermometer: Imagine a thermometer that ranges from 0 to 100 to assess the intensity of your anger. When you notice thoughts that fuel your anger, use this scale to quantify your emotion. This exercise helps you create emotional distance, allowing you to see your anger as a transient and manageable experience rather than an absolute reality. You can then compare your assessment with the actual intensity of the situation to downscale your reaction.

- Three Perspectives Exercise: To develop alternative interpretations, try considering the situation from your perspective, from the perspective of the other person involved, and from that of a neutral observer. This approach broadens your viewpoint, helping you see the situation from different angles and reducing the intensity of your anger. This exercise is especially useful when you feel your anger is taking over, as it forces you to question your initial perception.

- Mental Rewind: Mentally revisit the event that triggered your anger, and try to identify moments where you could have interpreted the situation differently. This exercise helps you see that your interpretations are not the only possible truth and that there are alternative ways of viewing the same situation. This can reduce resentment and help you develop greater cognitive flexibility.

- Cognitive De-escalation: When you notice thoughts that fuel your anger, consciously try to reduce their intensity. If you think, "This is a total disaster," try to modify it to "This is a difficult situation, but manageable." This technique helps you transform a potential emotional outburst into a more moderate and manageable response, preventing escalation.

- Self-Distancing Technique: When you feel anger rising, try to mentally distance yourself from the situation by imagining you are observing the scene as a third person. This exercise allows you to detach from the emotional intensity of the moment and assess the situation with greater objectivity, reducing the likelihood of an impulsive reaction.

- Emotion Diary: Keeping an emotion diary can be a powerful tool for managing anger. Each time you feel angry, write down your thoughts and feelings, describing what triggered the emotion, how you felt, and what you did in response. This process helps you vent and reflect, allowing you to identify recurring patterns and find more effective ways to handle similar situations in the future.

- Cultivating Self-Compassion: Often, anger is not only directed at others but also at yourself. In such cases, it's crucial to cultivate self-compassion. Instead of harshly judging yourself for your mistakes or how you reacted, try to treat yourself with the same kindness and understanding you would offer a close friend. This reduces the intensity of your anger and improves your overall emotional well-being.

- Positive Visualization: Before facing a situation you know might anger you, take a few minutes to imagine how you would like to react. Visualize yourself handling the situation with calm and resolve. This mental preparation can positively influence your real-life behavior, making you more capable of managing anger constructively.

- Attention Shifting: When you notice that you're starting to dwell on an offense or perceived injustice, try directing your attention to an activity you enjoy or find relaxing. This shift in focus doesn't immediately solve the problem but can help calm your mind and reduce the intensity of your anger, allowing you to approach the situation with greater clarity.

When practiced regularly, these strategies will help you develop greater awareness and control over your thoughts and reactions, enabling you to manage anger more effectively and constructively.

De-escalation Strategies

Managing anger effectively requires the use of strategies that can interrupt the emotional escalation before it spirals out of control. These techniques help calm you down, reframe your thoughts, and avoid impulsive reactions that could worsen the situation. Here are some innovative strategies for de-escalating anger:

- "Defusing" Technique: An effective strategy to reduce the intensity of anger is to "defuse" the situation. This can be done by changing the tone of the conversation, perhaps introducing an element of surprise or humor to break the tension. For example, you might say something unexpected and light that's unrelated to the conflict at hand. This can help "defuse" the tension and bring the discussion back to a more rational level.

- "Safe Word": Before entering potentially conflictual situations, agree with the person involved on a "safe word." When either of you says it, it means it's time to stop and take a break. This system allows both parties to step back from the emotional intensity and reflect before continuing the conversation.

- "Switch Tasking": When you feel anger rising, switching activities can help break the emotional cycle. For example, moving on to a completely different task, like tidying up a room or doing a quick physical exercise, can distract the mind and reduce adrenaline, allowing you to approach the situation more calmly afterward.

- "Self-Compassion Cycle": Anger is often accompanied by self-criticism and guilt. The "self-compassion cycle" technique involves taking a moment to acknowledge and accept your emotions without judgment. For instance, you might tell yourself, "It's normal to feel angry in this situation. I'm doing my best to handle it." This can help reduce the intensity of anger and develop a kinder attitude toward yourself.

- "Exploring Needs": In many cases, anger stems from unmet needs. A useful exercise is to ask yourself, "What need am I trying to express through anger?" It might be a need for respect, recognition, or safety. Recognizing these needs allows you to find more constructive ways to meet them, rather than letting anger take over.

- "Contrast Technique": Another useful technique is the "contrast" approach. Imagine how the situation could worsen if the anger continues to escalate, and then visualize how it could improve if you manage to stay calm. This technique helps you clearly see the consequences of your actions and choose a behavior that leads to a more positive outcome.

- "Refocusing on Solutions": When anger builds, it's easy to get stuck in the problem rather than looking for solutions. The "refocusing on solutions" technique involves consciously directing your thoughts toward practical solutions to the conflict at hand. Ask yourself, "What can I do now to improve the situation?" This shifts the focus from anger to resolution, reducing emotional intensity and promoting a quicker resolution.

- "Rooted Breathing Technique": A variation of diaphragmatic breathing is the "rooted breath." In addition to breathing deeply, imagine yourself rooting into the ground like a tree with deep roots. With each breath, feel these roots stabilizing you, keeping you steady and calm despite the emotional storm on the surface. This visualization, combined with deep breathing, can anchor you to the present moment and quickly calm your anger.

By regularly practicing these strategies, you can develop greater mastery over your emotional reactions and handle difficult situations with more balance and serenity.

Exercise 1: Anger Diary

For three episodes of anger, record the triggering situation, your thoughts, the intensity of your anger (on a scale of 1 to 10), and your actions.

Situation	Thoughts	Intensity (1-10)	Actions
Briefly describe the situation	*What thoughts did you have?*	*Rate the intensity of your anger*	*What did you do in response?*

Exercise 2: Challenging Angry Thoughts

Identify three common thoughts that fuel your anger. For each one, write a more balanced and rational response.

Angry Thought	Balanced Response

Exercise 3: Personal De-escalation Plan

Create a three-step plan to calm yourself when you feel anger rising. Include a relaxation technique, a calming affirmation, and a constructive action.

1. Relaxation Technique:

---

2. Calming Affirmation:

---

3. Constructive Action:

Chapter 16:

CBT for Self-Esteem and Self-Criticism

"You yourself, as much as anybody in the entire universe, deserve your love and affection." – Buddha

Self-esteem and self-criticism profoundly impact your daily life. This chapter will guide you through CBT techniques to recognize and modify the thoughts that undermine your self-esteem, helping you to develop a healthier and more compassionate relationship with yourself.

The Cognitive Model of Self-Esteem

In the CBT perspective, self-esteem represents the value you assign to yourself. It is not a fixed trait but a dynamic assessment influenced by your thoughts and experiences. Imagine self-esteem as an emotional thermometer that fluctuates based on your interpretations of events and your perception of yourself.

Your beliefs about yourself act as powerful filters. If you believe you are incompetent, you might interpret even your successes as mere luck or coincidence. These thoughts generate negative emotions, such as anxiety or sadness, which in turn influence your behavior. You might avoid challenges or opportunities, further reinforcing your initial belief of inadequacy.

Past experiences play a crucial role in shaping these beliefs. Constant criticism during childhood can instill the belief that you are never good enough. On the other hand, encouragement and support can nurture a sense of personal value. However, you are not condemned by your past experiences.

CBT offers tools to recognize and modify these deeply rooted beliefs. Start by observing your automatic thoughts in various situations. Notice how you react to compliments or criticisms. Do you feel worthy of praise, or do you tend to downplay your successes?

Unconscious Paradigms and Self-Esteem

"Unconscious paradigms" are deep-seated patterns that influence your perception of yourself and the world. These paradigms, often formed during childhood or through significant experiences, operate below the level of awareness, guiding your behavior and shaping your self-esteem. Here are some common examples of unconscious paradigms that can undermine self-esteem:

- *"I must be perfect to be loved"*: This paradigm leads you to believe that only perfection can guarantee acceptance and love from others. Every mistake or imperfection becomes a threat to your personal worth, leading to constant self-criticism and the fear of never being good enough.

- *"My worth depends on my achievements"*: When your sense of self-esteem is tied exclusively to your successes or failures, any defeat can be devastating. This paradigm pushes you to measure your personal value based on your achievements, neglecting other important aspects of your identity.

- *"I must never show weakness"*: This paradigm forces you to hide your vulnerabilities for fear of being judged or rejected. Suppressing emotions and not asking for help can isolate you from others and reinforce the belief that you must do everything on your own.

- *"Others are more important than me"*: If you believe that the needs and desires of others should always take priority over your own, you might sacrifice your well-being to please others. This attitude can lead to resentment and a diminished sense of self-worth.

- *"I must always be strong and independent"*: This paradigm pushes you to avoid showing any signs of weakness or dependence on others. While independence is a positive quality, believing that you must handle everything on your own can lead you to avoid meaningful relationships or not seek help when needed.

- *"My worth depends on others' opinions"*: If your self-esteem is primarily influenced by others' opinions, you will constantly seek external approval. This paradigm can lead to people-pleasing behavior and a lack of authenticity, as you strive to meet others' expectations rather than being yourself.

- *"I must never disappoint anyone"*: This paradigm leads you to prioritize others' needs over your own, avoiding situations where you might disappoint someone. While the desire to please others may seem altruistic, it can result in a life lived according to others' expectations, diminishing your self-esteem.

- *"I must never fail"*: The fear of failure can lead you to avoid risks or procrastinate, limiting your opportunities for personal growth. This paradigm prevents you from learning from your mistakes and seeing failure as a learning opportunity.

Remember, these beliefs are not immutable facts but hypotheses to be tested. CBT teaches you to challenge these assumptions and seek evidence that either confirms or disproves them. This process of inquiry can lead to a more balanced and realistic view of yourself.

Healthy self-esteem doesn't mean thinking you are perfect or superior to others. Rather, it means recognizing your intrinsic worth, regardless of external successes or failures. It means treating yourself with the same kindness and understanding that you would offer a good friend.

Working on self-esteem requires practice and patience. Thought patterns have formed over years and won't change overnight. However, with consistency and commitment, you can gradually replace old limiting beliefs with a more compassionate and realistic view of yourself.

Identifying and Challenging Negative Self-Talk

Identifying and challenging negative self-talk is essential for improving self-esteem and reducing self-criticism. Negative self-talk consists of automatic thoughts that often go unchecked and tend to undermine your confidence. Recognizing when you are engaging in excessively critical self-talk is the first step toward positive change.

Start by paying attention to moments when you feel down, frustrated, or anxious. These emotional states are often triggered by critical thoughts, such as "I'm not good enough," "I've failed again," or "I'm worthless." These thoughts can become so habitual that you accept them as truth without questioning them. It's helpful to pause and ask yourself, "What am I saying to myself right now?" This simple act of awareness allows you to identify negative self-talk.

Once you recognize the critical thought, it's important to examine its accuracy. Ask yourself, "Is this assessment really justified?" Often, negative thoughts are based on cognitive distortions, such as all-or-nothing thinking, where you see situations only in extreme terms without considering the nuances. For example, you might think, "I failed this project, so I'm a total failure," ignoring the times when you've succeeded. Another example is overgeneralization, where you take one negative event and conclude that everything will always go wrong. By examining these negative self-assessments, you can begin to see how they don't reflect reality but rather a distorted image of yourself.

To effectively challenge these thoughts, it's helpful to gather evidence that contradicts them. Consider, for example, your past experiences where you successfully dealt with similar situations. Ask yourself, "Is there really a basis for believing that I'm a failure?" or "Is it true that I'm worthless?" Try to recall specific examples that disprove these negative statements. This helps you develop a more balanced and realistic view of yourself.

The next step is to replace self-criticism with more compassionate self-talk. Instead of telling yourself, "I'm not good enough," try to reframe the thought into something kinder and more realistic, like "I'm doing my best, and that's okay." This doesn't mean ignoring areas where you can improve, but rather recognizing that your worth isn't dependent on your successes or failures. Practice self-compassion by speaking to yourself the way you would to a close friend. If a friend were struggling, you wouldn't harshly criticize them; you would offer words of encouragement and support. Do the same for yourself.

Another useful technique is to imagine how you would react if someone else were in your situation. Often, we are much harder on ourselves than we are on others. Ask yourself, "How would I respond if a friend told me what I'm thinking now?" This reflection can help you tone down self-criticism and develop a more compassionate and balanced approach toward yourself.

Challenging and changing negative self-talk requires practice and patience. Every time you successfully identify a critical thought and replace it with a more compassionate one, you take a step forward toward greater self-esteem and a healthier relationship with yourself. As you continue to practice, you will notice an improvement in your ability to manage self-criticism, leading to a more balanced and positive view of yourself.

Managing the Impact of External Criticism

External criticism can significantly impact your self-esteem and emotional well-being. Learning to handle criticism constructively is essential to maintaining a balanced view of yourself and ensuring that others' opinions don't define your worth.

Criticism, especially when perceived as unfair or excessive, can easily trigger negative emotions like anger, sadness, or anxiety. These reactions often stem from deep-seated beliefs, such as the idea that personal worth depends on others' approval. Recognizing that criticism doesn't define who you are, but is merely someone else's opinion, is the first step in reducing its impact.

Strategies for Managing External Criticism

Dealing with criticism in a healthy way takes practice and awareness. Here are some strategies to help you manage criticism without compromising your self-esteem:

- Separate the Message from the Messenger: Try to distinguish the criticism itself from the person delivering it. Ask yourself, "Is there something useful in this criticism?" even if it comes from someone you disagree with or don't respect. This allows you to assess the criticism more objectively.

- Acknowledge Constructive Content: Not all criticism is destructive. Some can offer valuable insights for personal growth. Try to identify if there's an aspect of the criticism that can help you improve or see a situation from a different perspective.

- Set Personal Boundaries: It's important to know when criticism is unfair or harmful and when it's time to protect your self-esteem. If criticism is repetitive, excessively negative, or expressed in a rude manner, it's useful to set clear boundaries. You might say something like, "I appreciate your feedback, but I would prefer to discuss it in a more constructive way."

- Avoid Personalizing Criticism: Not all criticism is about you as a person. Often, people express criticism based on their own experiences, emotions, or insecurities. Ask yourself, "Does this criticism really reflect a shortcoming of mine, or could it be more related to the other person's experience?"

- Respond Calmly and Rationally: Take a moment to breathe and reflect before responding to criticism. Avoiding immediate reactions gives you time to consider a more balanced and less emotional response, reducing the chances of escalating the conflict.

- Develop Self-Validation: Strengthening your ability to self-validate helps you maintain confidence, even when faced with criticism. Remind yourself of your values, strengths, and achievements. This allows you to balance external criticism with a strong internal sense of your worth.

A balanced perspective on criticism allows you to grow without compromising your self-esteem. View criticism as a learning opportunity rather than a personal attack. Cultivate the ability to listen to constructive feedback without getting lost in negative details or feeling overwhelmed.

No one is immune to criticism, and the ability to handle it is a skill that develops over time. Every criticism can be seen as an opportunity to strengthen your resilience, reinforce your personal boundaries, and continue to grow with confidence and security.

Techniques to Increase Self-Efficacy

Self-efficacy, a concept introduced by psychologist Albert Bandura, refers to your belief in your ability to organize and carry out the actions necessary to achieve specific goals. It plays a fundamental role in human behavior, as it influences your motivation, perseverance, and ability to face challenges. Self-efficacy is closely related to self-esteem, but the two concepts are not the same. While self-esteem concerns the overall value you attribute to yourself, self-efficacy focuses on your perception of your abilities in specific contexts. For example, you may have high self-esteem overall but feel ineffective in certain areas, such as public speaking or tackling certain professional challenges.

Increasing your self-efficacy will not only help you feel more confident in your abilities but can also contribute to boosting your self-esteem. Achieving concrete results in areas of competence strengthens your sense of personal worth. Improving self-efficacy requires conscious effort, using strategies that help you develop a more positive outlook on your abilities.

The first step to increasing your self-efficacy is becoming aware of your strengths. Take the time to reflect on your past successes: which skills helped you achieve those results? Asking for feedback from trusted people, such as friends, colleagues, or mentors, can help you gain an external perspective on your strengths and how to best leverage them.

Once you've identified your strengths, it's important to value them. Don't just acknowledge them—actively use them in your daily life. For example, if you are particularly good at problem-solving, apply this skill to new situations to build your confidence in your abilities. This will help you develop an increasingly positive perception of what you're capable of achieving.

To strengthen your self-efficacy, it's crucial to set realistic goals. A common mistake is setting goals that are too ambitious or vague, which can lead to frustration and lower your confidence in your abilities. On the other hand, setting clear, specific, and achievable goals will help you build confidence in your skills.

You can follow the SMART method when setting your goals: make sure they are Specific, Measurable, Achievable, Relevant, and Time-bound. Defining SMART goals will give you a clear direction and help you monitor your progress more effectively. For example, if your goal is to improve your public speaking skills, you might start with a short presentation in a safe environment within a month, gradually moving on to more complex challenges.

Achieving small, incremental goals will help reinforce your sense of personal efficacy. Each success, no matter how small, will create a positive feedback loop: it will strengthen your belief that you can take on increasingly complex challenges. Remember to celebrate your successes and acknowledge their value: each goal you achieve is a stepping stone toward enhancing your self-efficacy.

As you work on increasing your self-efficacy, it's important to take a moment to reflect on your current strengths and goals. Consider the following questions to help guide your thoughts and reinforce your progress:

- *What are your most evident strengths?*

- *How are you using them to tackle everyday challenges?*

- *Do you feel confident in setting goals that are both achievable and motivating?*

- *What can you do today to build a small success that increases your confidence in your abilities?*

- *What could you do tomorrow to further expand your skills and enhance your sense of personal effectiveness?*

Exercise 1: Internal Dialogue Log

For 7 days, track your self-critical thoughts. Whenever you catch yourself thinking negatively about yourself, write it down. Then, respond with a more compassionate thought, as if you were talking to a friend instead of yourself.

Day	Situation	Self-Critical Thought	Compassionate Response
	During a work presentation	*I did a terrible job, I'm not good at public speaking.*	*It's normal to feel nervous. You prepared well and did your best, which is what matters.*

Exercise 2: My Positive Qualities

List 10 of your positive qualities. For each quality, write a concrete example of a situation where you demonstrated it.

Quality	Example
Empathy	*I listened attentively to a colleague in distress and offered my support, helping them feel understood and less alone.*
Determination	*I persevered on an important project despite initial difficulties and successfully completed it.*

Exercise 3: Challenging Limiting Beliefs

Identify a limiting belief you have about yourself. List the evidence that supports this belief and the evidence that contradicts it. Finally, write a new, more balanced belief that better reflects reality.

Example:

Limiting Belief: "I'm not good at time management."

Supporting Evidence	Contradictory Evidence
I've often delivered projects late.	*I met the deadlines for my last two important projects.*
I tend to procrastinate on difficult tasks.	*I've started planning my work better with a weekly schedule.*

New Balanced Belief: "I can improve my time management by focusing on effective planning and continuing to work steadily on my projects."

Limiting Belief: _____

Supporting Evidence	Contradictory Evidence

New Balanced Belief: _____

Chapter 17:

CBT in Relationships

"The meeting of two personalities is like the contact of two chemical substances: if there is any reaction, both are transformed." – Carl Jung

Relationships shape our lives, influencing our happiness and well-being. This chapter explores how Cognitive Behavioral Therapy (CBT) can enhance your connections with others. You'll discover ways to identify and modify interpersonal patterns, communicate more effectively, and cultivate deeper connections.

Interpersonal Patterns

Interpersonal patterns are mental models that guide how you interact with others. They are formed through past experiences and profoundly influence your current relationships. These patterns act as filters, shaping your perceptions, expectations, and reactions in social interactions.

Early life experiences, especially those with parents or caregivers, play a crucial role in forming these patterns. A child raised by overprotective parents might develop a pattern of viewing the world as a dangerous place, leading them to constantly seek reassurance in adult relationships. Conversely, someone who has experienced abandonment might develop a pattern of distrust, struggling to form close bonds out of fear of being hurt again.

Once formed, these patterns tend to perpetuate themselves. They influence how you interpret others' actions and choose to respond, often creating a cycle that reinforces your initial beliefs. For example, if you have a rejection pattern, you might interpret a neutral comment from a friend as criticism, reacting with anger or withdrawal. This reaction could indeed lead to your friend distancing themselves, reinforcing your initial belief of being rejected.

Identifying your interpersonal patterns requires careful observation of your recurring thoughts, emotions, and behaviors in relationships. Pay attention to situations where you react disproportionately or find yourself involved in familiar but problematic dynamics. These moments often signal the presence of an underlying pattern.

A useful exercise is to trace the history of your significant relationships, looking for common themes. Do you notice recurring patterns in your romantic relationships? Are there roles you tend to take on repeatedly in friendships? These patterns can reveal the underlying schemas that influence your interactions.

Awareness of your patterns is the first step toward change. Once identified, you can begin to challenge them and test new ways of interacting. This process requires practice and patience but can lead to more satisfying and authentic relationships.

Assertive Communication

Assertive communication is a fundamental skill in CBT for improving interpersonal relationships. It allows you to express your thoughts, feelings, and needs clearly and respectfully, without overpowering others or diminishing yourself. This skill balances the expression of your own rights with respect for those of others. In CBT, assertiveness is based on the principle that every individual has the right to express themselves, as long as it is done in a respectful manner. This approach is distinct from both passive communication, which sacrifices one's own needs, and aggressive communication, which disregards the rights of others. Assertiveness requires awareness of your own thoughts and feelings, as well as the ability to express them constructively.

To communicate assertively, start by observing your internal dialogues. Often, negative automatic thoughts can hinder assertive expression. Phrases like "I don't have the right to ask for this" or "If I express my disagreement, the other person will get angry" may lead you to avoid direct communication. Challenge these thoughts by examining the evidence for and against them. Below are some assertive communication techniques you can use in everyday life:

1. The DESC Model: This technique is useful for structuring your message clearly and respectfully. DESC stands for Describe, Express, Specify, and Consequences:

    o Describe: Start by describing the situation objectively, without assigning blame. For example: "When I don't receive feedback on my reports..."

    o Express: Express your feelings about the situation: "...I feel frustrated and unappreciated."

    o Specify: Specify what you would like to change: "I would appreciate receiving feedback so I can know if I'm on the right track."

    o Consequences: Indicate the positive consequences of the requested change: "This way, I can improve my work and contribute more effectively to the project."

2. Using "I" Statements: Avoid blaming or pointing fingers. Instead of saying, "You make me angry," try "I feel angry when...". This approach reduces the likelihood of the other person becoming defensive and opens up constructive dialogue.

3. Body Language: Body language is crucial in supporting assertive communication. Maintain eye contact to show confidence and sincerity. Use a calm but firm tone of

voice to express seriousness without aggression. An open posture, with relaxed shoulders and visible hands, conveys openness and willingness to engage. Avoid gestures like crossing your arms, which can appear defensive or hostile.

4. Active Listening: Being assertive isn't just about expressing your own needs, but also about actively listening to those of others. Practice reflective listening, where you repeat or rephrase what the other person has said to ensure you understand correctly. This not only shows respect but also facilitates conflict resolution.

5. The Broken Record Technique: When you're in a situation where the other person tries to divert the conversation or avoid addressing your request, calmly repeat your main point. For example: "I understand you're busy, but it's important that we discuss this. I'd like to know what you think about my work." This technique helps you stay focused on your message without becoming aggressive.

6. Dealing with Rejection: Being assertive also includes knowing how to handle rejection. If your request is not accepted, respect the other person's response, but continue to express your needs clearly. For example: "I understand that you can't help me right now. Could we revisit this issue next week?"

7. Learning to Say "No": Saying "no" assertively is essential to protect your personal boundaries. You can decline a request in a respectful but firm way, such as: "I appreciate that you asked for my help, but I can't commit to this project right now."

8. The Sandwich Technique: This technique involves placing a criticism or difficult request between two positive comments. Start with a recognition or appreciation, then express your concern or request, and end with another positive observation. For example: "I really value your dedication to the project. I'd like to discuss some changes that could further improve our work. I'm confident that with your skills, we can achieve excellent results."

9. Strategic Pause: When you feel overwhelmed or emotionally involved in a discussion, a short pause can help you gather your thoughts and respond more balanced. This is not a sign of weakness but a strategy to keep the conversation constructive. You can say: "I need a moment to reflect on what's been said, let's talk again shortly."

10. Handling Criticism Assertively: When you receive criticism, instead of reacting defensively, listen carefully and assess whether there's something useful in the feedback. If the criticism is justified, thank the person and ask for suggestions on how to improve. If you believe the criticism is unfounded, express your point of view calmly and respectfully: "I understand your perspective, but I see the situation differently. Here's how I interpret it..."

Practicing these techniques in daily situations will help you improve your assertive communication. Over time, you'll become more confident in handling social interactions, creating more balanced and fulfilling relationships.

Conflict Management

The CBT approach to conflict resolution is based on the premise that it's not the events themselves that cause stress, but the interpretations we give them. In a conflict situation, your automatic thoughts can intensify negative emotions and lead to impulsive reactions. Learning to recognize and challenge these thoughts is the first step toward effective conflict management.

When you find yourself in disagreement with someone, take a moment to observe your thoughts. You might notice catastrophic thinking like "This will ruin our relationship" or excessive generalizations such as "We can never get along." These thoughts fuel anxiety and anger, making peaceful resolution more difficult.

Conflict Management Techniques:

1. Cognitive Restructuring: To challenge negative thoughts, ask yourself, "What evidence do I have that this thought is true?" or "Are there other possible interpretations of the situation?" This cognitive restructuring process helps you view the conflict more objectively and maintain the calm necessary for a constructive resolution.

2. Focus on the Specific Issue: Avoid broadening the conflict to unrelated issues. Clearly define the point of disagreement and keep the discussion centered on it. This approach helps prevent escalation and keeps the focus on solving the problem.

3. Alternative Perspective Technique: Try to view the situation from the other person's perspective, imagining how they might interpret the same situation. This exercise not only helps generate empathy but can also reveal new resolution possibilities that may not be immediately obvious.

4. Emotional De-escalation Technique: If emotions are running high, use relaxation techniques like deep breathing or grounding to calm your nervous system. This allows you to return to the conflict with a clearer and less reactive mind.

5. Mind Mapping: Instead of discussing in a linear fashion, try visualizing the problem as a mind map. Write down the central issue and draw branches with possible solutions, along with their pros and cons. This visual approach can help you see the issue from different angles and find creative solutions.

6. Reflection Time Technique: After a discussion or conflict, take time to reflect on what was said and how it was communicated. This moment of reflection allows you to

identify any communication errors or points that may have been misunderstood, offering an opportunity to clarify and resolve any outstanding issues.

7. Managing Pride: Often, pride can hinder conflict resolution. Work on recognizing when pride is influencing your responses and learn to set aside ego for the sake of the relationship and finding a solution.

8. Strategic Silence Technique: Master the art of strategic silence. In some situations, silence can be a powerful tool to allow the other person to reflect on what has been said, reducing tension and opening up space for understanding.

9. Positive Scenario Visualization: Before addressing a conflict, imagine how you would like the conversation to go. Visualize a calm, respectful, and constructive discussion. This technique mentally prepares you to maintain a positive and proactive attitude during the confrontation.

10. Learning from Conflict: After resolving a conflict, reflect on what you have learned. Ask yourself, "What worked well?" and "What can I do differently next time?" This approach helps you grow and improve your conflict management skills for the future.

Enhancing Intimacy and Connection

Emotional intimacy is fundamental to building deep and fulfilling relationships. It is based on the ability to share your deepest thoughts and feelings with another person, creating an authentic bond. Your cognitions, or thought patterns, directly influence this ability, determining how comfortable you feel opening up and receiving others' openness.

Exploring and Modifying Limiting Beliefs

CBT offers practical tools to examine and modify the beliefs that hinder intimacy. A useful exercise is targeted self-observation: for one week, pay particular attention to moments when you feel the desire to emotionally connect with someone. When this desire arises, observe what happens internally: what thoughts come to mind? For example, you might think, "I can't fully trust them," or "If I open up, I might get hurt." Also, notice any physical sensations, such as muscle tension or a racing heartbeat, which may indicate emotional resistance. For example, if you feel nervous when a friend approaches you for a deep conversation, take note of what you're thinking at that moment and reflect on how those thoughts might be influencing your reaction.

Reflecting on Past Experiences

Barriers to intimacy are often rooted in past experiences. Tracing an "intimacy timeline" can help you identify significant events that have influenced how you relate to others. For instance, if you've experienced betrayal in the past, you might find yourself more reluctant to open up in current relationships. Identifying these events allows you to understand how they have shaped your current beliefs and behaviors. Once you've identified these patterns, you can begin to challenge them, asking yourself if they are still relevant or if they can be replaced with more constructive beliefs.

Embracing Vulnerability

Vulnerability is at the heart of intimacy. Many avoid it out of fear of being hurt or rejected, but it's the act of being vulnerable that creates deep connections. A gradual approach can help you overcome this fear: start by sharing thoughts or feelings that are slightly outside your comfort zone. You might say something simple yet personal, like "I feel nervous talking about this, but I think it's important." Observe the reactions of both yourself and the other person, noticing how openness often encourages a reciprocal response. For example, try sharing a recent experience that made you happy, even if it seems trivial, and see how this openness encourages the other person to do the same.

Practicing Mindful Presence

"Mindful presence" is another powerful tool for enhancing intimacy. In your daily interactions, make an effort to be fully present. This means not only actively listening to the other person's words but also tuning into their body language, tone of voice, and micro-expressions. Avoid distractions like your phone or thoughts about what to say next. Being truly present communicates to the other person that you value them, strengthening the emotional bond. For example, during a conversation with a partner, put away your phone and focus entirely on what they're saying, responding with questions that show your genuine interest.

Valuing Small Daily Actions

Intimacy is not built solely through grand gestures or deep conversations but also through small daily actions. A sincere smile, a gesture of affection, or simply remembering to ask, "How are you really doing?" can have a significant impact. These small actions show the other person that you care about their happiness and well-being. For instance, sending an encouraging message to a friend before an important event can strengthen your bond, showing that you care about them.

Considering Intimacy as a Skill to Develop

Finally, it's helpful to view intimacy as a skill that can be developed and refined over time. Set concrete goals to improve your ability to connect emotionally, such as openly expressing one emotion each day or dedicating daily time to meaningful conversations. For example, you could commit to sharing a thought or feeling with a friend or partner every day for a week, monitoring how this practice affects your relationship. With time and practice, these habits will become a natural part of your way of relating, leading to deeper and more satisfying relationships.

In this way, intimacy becomes not just an aspect of relationships but a daily practice that strengthens your connections with others and enriches your emotional life.

Exercise 1: Key Relationship Analysis

Reflect on your most important relationships. For each one, identify a recurring thought and a typical behavioral reaction.

Relationship	Recurring Thought	Typical Reaction

Exercise 2: Assertive Communication Practice

Choose a situation where you want to communicate assertively. Use the format "I feel... when... because... and I would like..."

Choose a situation:

_____

_____

I feel...

when...

because...

and I would like...

Exercise 3: Restructuring Relationship Thoughts

Identify recurring negative thoughts in an important relationship. Challenge each one using CBT techniques and write a more balanced thought.

Negative Thought	Challenge	Balanced Thought

Chapter 18:

CBT for Habits and Addictions

"Habit is the intersection of knowledge (what to do), skill (how to do), and desire (want to do)." - Stephen Covey

This chapter explores the application of CBT in addressing dysfunctional habits and addictions. The goal is to provide you with practical tools to understand and modify problematic behaviors, offering a structured approach to developing healthier habits.

The Cognitive-Behavioral Model of Addictions

The cognitive-behavioral model of addictions provides a comprehensive perspective on the mechanisms that fuel and sustain addictive behaviors. This approach is based on the premise that thoughts, emotions, and behaviors are interconnected, influencing each other in a cycle that can perpetuate addiction.

At the core of this model is the addiction cycle, which develops through a series of interconnected phases. It begins with a trigger, which can be internal (such as a negative emotional state) or external (such as seeing an object associated with the addiction). This trigger activates automatic thoughts and deep-seated beliefs related to the substance or behavior involved in the addiction.

Automatic thoughts are quick, often unconscious, and tend to be distorted or irrational. In the context of addictions, they might take forms such as "I need this to feel better" or "I can't handle stress without resorting to...". These thoughts are supported by deeper beliefs, such as "I am weak" or "The world is too hard to face when sober."

These thoughts and beliefs generate intense emotions, which in turn fuel the desire to engage in the addictive behavior. The resulting craving leads to action, reinforcing the cycle through the temporary relief or pleasure obtained. However, this relief is often followed by feelings of guilt or shame, which paradoxically can become new triggers, perpetuating the cycle.

The role of automatic thoughts and beliefs in maintaining addictions is crucial. These cognitive structures act as filters through which we interpret experiences, influencing our emotional and behavioral responses. In the case of addictions, they can lead to cognitive distortions such as:

1. Minimization: "It's not that bad; I can quit whenever I want."

2. Rationalization: "I deserve this after such a stressful day."

3. Dichotomous thinking: "I've already given in once; I might as well continue."

These cognitive distortions contribute to maintaining addictive behavior, creating a system of self-justification that makes change difficult.

The interaction between cognitive, emotional, and behavioral factors in habits is complex and multidirectional. Thoughts influence emotions, which in turn drive behaviors. At the same time, behaviors can reinforce certain beliefs and generate new emotions, creating a feedback loop.

For example, the thought "I can't face this situation without drinking" may generate anxiety, leading to alcohol consumption. The temporary relief obtained reinforces the initial belief, increasing the likelihood of turning to alcohol in similar future situations.

CBT aims to break this cycle by intervening at various points:

1. Identifying and modifying automatic thoughts and dysfunctional beliefs.

2. Developing alternative coping strategies to manage difficult emotions.

3. Modifying behaviors through techniques such as gradual exposure and positive reinforcement.

4. Teaching problem-solving skills and stress management.

Understanding this model is the first step in effectively applying CBT techniques to the treatment of addictions. In the following sections, we will explore specific tools for identifying triggers, managing cravings, and preventing relapses, based on this understanding of the addiction cycle.

Identifying Triggers and Problematic Behaviors

Accurately identifying triggers and problematic behaviors is a crucial step in changing dysfunctional habits or addictions. This awareness phase allows you to interrupt the automatic cycle that sustains the undesired behavior.

Triggers can be classified into two main categories: internal and external. Internal triggers include emotional states, physical sensations, and thoughts, while external triggers refer to environmental situations, people, or objects.

To identify your internal triggers, pay attention to your moods and physical sensations before engaging in the problematic behavior. You might notice that anxiety, sadness, or boredom often precede the urge to drink, smoke, or overeat. Physical sensations such as muscle tension or headaches can also serve as triggers.

Daily monitoring is an effective tool for this identification. Keep a journal where you note:

- The moment you feel the urge

- What you were doing

- How you felt emotionally and physically

- The thoughts that crossed your mind

To effectively address these issues, it's essential to employ specific techniques that help in recognizing and managing both internal and external triggers, as well as understanding the underlying patterns that drive these behaviors. Below, we'll explore several key techniques that can assist in this process.

Environmental Scanning

For external triggers, closely observe your surroundings when the urge arises. You may discover that certain places, times of day, or social groups are associated with the behavior you wish to change.

A useful technique for identifying these external triggers is "environmental scanning." Spend a few minutes each day consciously observing your environment, noting the elements that might trigger your desire. This practice increases your awareness of potential external triggers.

Functional Analysis of Habitual or Addictive Behaviors

Functional analysis is a structured method to understand the role that the problematic behavior plays in your life. This approach examines the antecedents (what happens before), the behavior itself, and the consequences (what happens after).

To conduct a functional analysis:

- Describe the specific behavior you want to change.

- Identify the immediate antecedents: what happens right before the behavior?

- List the short-term consequences: what immediate benefits do you get?

- Consider the long-term consequences: what are the negative effects over time?

This process helps you understand the functions that the behavior serves in your life. Often, you will find that the problematic behavior is a maladaptive attempt to meet a legitimate need, such as relieving stress or seeking social connection.

Once these functions are identified, you can begin to develop healthier alternative strategies to meet the same needs. For example, if you drink to reduce social anxiety, you might explore relaxation techniques or communication skills as alternatives.

Mapping Thought-Emotion-Behavior Patterns

Mapping thought-emotion-behavior patterns allows you to visualize the connections between these elements, offering a deeper understanding of your addiction cycle.

One effective technique is the "ABC diagram":

- A (Antecedent): The triggering event or situation
- B (Belief): The thoughts and beliefs that are activated
- C (Consequence): The resulting emotions and behaviors

To create your ABC diagram:

1. Start by identifying a specific event that triggered the problematic behavior.
2. List the automatic thoughts you had in that situation.
3. Describe the emotions you experienced.
4. Note the resulting behavior.
5. Reflect on the short-term and long-term consequences of this behavior.

Repeat this process for several episodes to identify recurring patterns. You may notice that certain types of thoughts consistently lead to specific emotions and problematic behaviors.

Behavioral Chain Analysis

Behavioral chain analysis is a technique that breaks down the process leading to the problematic behavior into a series of small steps. This method helps you identify intervention points where you can interrupt the chain before reaching the undesired behavior.

For example, a behavioral chain might look like this:

- Argument with partner → Feeling of frustration → Thought "I can't handle this" → Urge to drink → Go to the bar → Excessive drinking

By identifying these steps, you can develop early intervention strategies. You might work on communication techniques to manage conflicts, practice cognitive restructuring to challenge the thought "I can't handle this," or plan alternative activities when you feel the urge to drink.

Accurately identifying triggers and mapping thought-emotion-behavior patterns are crucial steps in breaking the cycle of addiction. These techniques provide a solid foundation for developing more effective coping strategies and creating a personalized action plan for change.

Managing Cravings

Cravings—those intense desires that seem to consume you from within—are often at the core of addictions and problematic habits. However, you are not powerless against them. In fact, with the right strategies, you can learn to ride the wave of desire without being overwhelmed. Let's explore how you can do this.

We begin with the power of your mind. Cognitive strategies are like a gym for your brain, training it to see cravings in a new light. Imagine yourself as a scientist observing a fascinating phenomenon. When you feel a craving, rather than fighting it, observe it. Notice how it manifests in your body. Maybe you feel a tingling in your hands or tension in your stomach. Describe it to yourself as if you were taking notes for an experiment. This simple act of observation can create distance between you and the craving, reducing its power over you.

And if observation isn't enough? This is where visualization comes into play. Imagine your craving as a wave in the ocean. You see it growing in the distance, approaching, and getting taller. But instead of letting it crash over you, picture yourself riding it confidently. You climb to the crest, maintain your balance, and watch as the wave crashes onto the shore while you remain standing. This image reminds you that, like waves, cravings pass.

As you face these intense moments, the way you talk to yourself can make all the difference. Prepare some encouraging phrases in advance. They could be as simple as "This will pass" or more personal like "Every time I resist, I get stronger." Repeat these to yourself like a mantra when the craving hits.

Sometimes, the key isn't to fight the craving but to simply buy yourself some time. This is where the 5-minute rule comes into play. When you feel the urge to give in, make a deal with yourself: wait for just 5 minutes. It doesn't sound like much, right? But during those 5 minutes, your job is to distract yourself. Take a quick walk, call a friend, solve a puzzle. Often, by the end of those 5 minutes, you'll find the urgency has subsided.

Speaking of distractions, have you ever heard of the HALT technique? Before giving in to a craving, stop and ask yourself: Am I Hungry? Angry? Lonely? Tired? Often, our most intense desires mask more basic needs. Identifying and addressing these needs can extinguish the craving at its source.

But what happens when craving-related thoughts seem to take over? This is where cognitive restructuring comes into play. Think of these thoughts as old, shaky buildings. Your task is to examine them closely, see if they really hold up, and if necessary, rebuild them on stronger foundations.

When you catch yourself thinking, "I can't resist," stop. Ask yourself: is that really true? Have there been times when you resisted before? How did you feel afterward? Often, by examining these thoughts in the light of reality, you'll find they're less solid than they seemed.

And instead of saying, "I need this to feel better," try asking yourself, "What other ways do I have to improve my mood?" You might be surprised by the alternatives that come to mind.

One last powerful technique is the "fast forward" method. The next time you feel a craving, instead of focusing on the present moment, project your mind into the future. How will you feel an hour after giving in? And tomorrow? And a week from now? Compare these feelings with how you would feel if you resisted. This broader perspective can give you the motivation you need to overcome the difficult moment.

Remember, managing cravings is like learning to play an instrument or speak a new language. At first, it may seem difficult and unnatural. But with practice, it will become easier. Every time you apply these techniques, you are building new connections in your brain, strengthening your ability to resist.

Don't expect perfection. There will be days when these techniques seem to work perfectly, and others when you struggle. The important thing is to keep practicing, be kind to yourself, and remember that every small step is progress toward the person you want to become.

A Step-by-Step Approach to Relapse Prevention

Preventing relapse is a process that requires careful planning, awareness, and a well-structured strategy. This step-by-step approach will guide you through the essential phases to reduce the risk of relapse and effectively handle it if it occurs.

Step 1: Identify High-Risk Situations

The first step is to recognize situations where you are most vulnerable to relapse. These situations can include specific contexts, emotional states, or events that increase the likelihood of returning to problematic behaviors. Here's how you can do it:

1. Reflect on your past experiences: Note the moments when you experienced a relapse or felt a strong urge to give in. Identify the triggers, such as stressful situations, people involved, or dominant emotions.

2. Create a list of high-risk situations: Write down the circumstances that make you more vulnerable. This list will serve as a reference for preparing your prevention strategies.

3. Monitor your emotional state: Keep track of your daily moods and feelings to identify any patterns or signals that might indicate an impending relapse.

Step 2: Develop Coping Strategies for Difficult Situations

Once you've identified the high-risk situations, it's essential to develop strategies to handle them. Here's how to proceed:

1. Plan ahead: For each high-risk situation, devise a specific strategy. For example, if you know that evenings alone put you at risk, plan activities that keep you occupied and away from the problematic behavior.

2. Learn stress management techniques: Equip yourself with tools like deep breathing, meditation, or physical exercise. These techniques will help you manage intense emotions without resorting to old behaviors.

3. Create an "emergency kit": Prepare an action plan that includes contact information for supportive people, activities that help you relax or distract yourself, and positive affirmations to repeat during a crisis.

Step 3: Prepare a Plan of Action for Managing Relapses

Even with the best strategies, relapses can happen. Here's how to prepare:

1. Accept that relapses can occur: Prevention doesn't mean eliminating the risk entirely. View relapses as part of the change process, not as failures.

2. Analyze the relapse without judgment: If a relapse occurs, analyze what happened. What factors contributed? What could you have done differently? Use this information to strengthen your prevention plan.

3. Adopt a self-compassionate attitude: Treat yourself with kindness and understanding. Relapses are opportunities to learn and improve. Acknowledge your progress and continue working toward your goals.

Step 4: Reinforce Your Commitment

The final step involves maintaining your long-term commitment:

1. Regularly review and update your plan: As you progress, revisit your prevention plan and update your strategies based on new insights and experiences.

2. Acknowledge your successes: Celebrate your progress, even the small victories. Every step forward is an achievement that brings you closer to your goal of maintaining healthier habits.

3. Continue practicing your strategies: Relapse prevention requires constant practice. Keep using your coping techniques and applying the strategies you've developed, making them a permanent part of your daily routine.

Exercise 1: Trigger Diary

For one week, record moments when you feel the urge to engage in the habit or behavior you want to change. Note the situation, your thoughts, emotions, and the intensity of the craving.

Day	Situation	Thoughts	Emotions	Intensity (1-10)
Mon				
Tue				
Wed				
Thu				
Fri				
Sat				
Sun				

Exercise 2: Craving Management Plan:

Create a three-step plan to manage moments of intense desire. Include a distraction technique, a coping affirmation, and a healthy alternative action.

Distraction Technique:

_____

_____

Coping Affirmation:

_____

_____

Healthy Alternative Action:

_____

_____

Exercise 3: Restructuring Dependency Thoughts

Identify three common thoughts that support your habit. For each, write a healthier and more realistic response.

Dependency Thought	Restructured Thought

PART 3 – ACT

Welcome to the final part of our book, focusing on Acceptance and Commitment Therapy (ACT). ACT is a unique approach that combines mindfulness strategies with commitment and behavior-change techniques. Rather than trying to change your thoughts directly, ACT teaches you to change your relationship with your thoughts and feelings. In this section, you'll learn about psychological flexibility, cognitive defusion, and how to live a values-driven life. We'll explore how accepting difficult thoughts and feelings, rather than fighting them, can paradoxically lead to greater peace and fulfillment. The exercises in this part will help you clarify your personal values, develop mindfulness skills, and take committed action towards a rich and meaningful life, even in the face of challenges.

Chapter 19:

Introduction to ACT

"Between stimulus and response there is a space. In that space is our power to choose our response. In our response lies our growth and our freedom." - Viktor E. Frankl

In this chapter, you will explore Acceptance and Commitment Therapy (ACT), an innovative approach to psychotherapy. You will learn about its origins, core principles, and how it differs from other therapies. I will guide you through the six central processes of ACT and demonstrate how they work together to develop psychological flexibility.

Origins and Development of ACT

Acceptance and Commitment Therapy (ACT), developed in the 1980s by Steven C. Hayes, represents an innovative response to the challenges of modern psychotherapy. This therapy is rooted in radical behaviorism and relational frame theory (RFT), a complex theory of language and cognition.

Hayes, observing patients struggling against their negative thoughts, questioned whether there might be a different approach to psychological distress. This reflection led to the development of a therapeutic model that emphasizes the context and function of thought rather than its content.

The core principle of this approach is revolutionary: psychological suffering often arises from attempts to control or eliminate unpleasant internal experiences. Instead of fighting against difficult thoughts and emotions, ACT encourages you to accept them as a natural part of the human experience. This isn't about resignation; it's about learning to coexist with difficulties while moving toward what truly matters to you.

Six fundamental processes form the heart of this therapy:

1. Acceptance: Embracing experiences without judgment.

    o Practical Example: Imagine being stuck in traffic, feeling your irritation grow. Instead of fighting this emotion or trying to distract yourself, ACT invites you to accept it. You might say to yourself, "I'm feeling irritated. It's an unpleasant sensation, but I can handle it." By accepting the emotion without trying to change it, you reduce its power over you and free yourself to choose how to respond.

2. Cognitive Defusion: Distancing yourself from thoughts without getting entangled in them.

   o Practical Example: Suppose the thought "I'm a failure" comes to mind after making a mistake at work. Instead of taking it as a fact, you can practice defusion. Repeat the thought to yourself, but sing it to a familiar tune or imagine writing it on a cloud that then drifts away. This helps you see the thought for what it is: a product of the mind, not an absolute truth.

3. Self as Context: Recognizing a broader, more flexible sense of self.

   o Practical Example: Imagine feeling inadequate during a meeting. Instead of fully identifying with this sensation ("I am inadequate"), ACT encourages you to see the self as the context in which these feelings appear. You might say, "I'm having the thought that I'm inadequate, but I'm not just this thought." This allows you to view yourself as a complex, multidimensional being capable of experiencing a wide range of emotions and thoughts.

4. Contact with the Present Moment: Fully experiencing the current moment.

   o Practical Example: You're in an important conversation, but your mind keeps drifting to a problem at work. Instead of letting the distraction take over, practice present-moment awareness by focusing on your breath and gently bringing your attention back to the conversation. Notice the other person's facial expressions, the tone of their voice, and what they are saying. This helps you stay present and engaged in the interaction.

5. Values: Identifying what is truly important to you.

   o Practical Example: You might feel uncertain about a major life decision, like changing careers. ACT invites you to reflect on your core values. Ask yourself, "What is truly important to me in life? What kind of person do I want to be?" If personal growth is a primary value for you, you might decide to pursue the career change despite the uncertainty, as it aligns with what matters most to you.

6. Committed Action: Acting in line with your values, despite challenges.

   o Practical Example: After identifying health as an important value, you decide to start exercising regularly. Even on days when you feel unmotivated or tired, ACT encourages you to take committed action, such as going for a walk, because it aligns with your value of taking care of your body.

These processes work together to promote psychological flexibility—the ability to stay anchored in the present and adapt your behavior based on your values.

This approach significantly differs from traditional cognitive-behavioral therapy (CBT). While CBT often aims to modify the content of negative thoughts, Acceptance and Commitment Therapy focuses on changing your relationship with those thoughts. It doesn't seek to eliminate difficult emotions but rather to create space for them while you move toward a richer and more meaningful life.

A distinctive aspect of this therapy is its emphasis on personal values. Rather than focusing solely on symptom reduction, ACT encourages you to reflect on what is truly important to you and to align your actions in that direction. This values-based approach offers intrinsic motivation for change, going beyond mere symptom relief.

The methodology includes a variety of experiential techniques, such as metaphors, mindfulness exercises, and practical activities. These techniques aim to help you directly experience key concepts rather than just discussing them intellectually.

Finally, this therapeutic model adopts a contextual view of human behavior. It recognizes that psychological problems do not exist in isolation but are intertwined with an individual's cultural, social, and personal context. This holistic approach allows for deeper understanding and more targeted interventions.

Acceptance and Commitment Therapy continues to evolve, with research demonstrating its effectiveness across a wide range of psychological issues, from depression and anxiety to eating disorders and chronic pain. Its flexibility and focus on personal values make it an adaptable and powerful approach, capable of offering new perspectives and tools for facing the challenges of modern life.

Psychological Flexibility

Psychological flexibility is a core concept in Acceptance and Commitment Therapy (ACT) and refers to the ability to adapt to life's changes while maintaining a balance between your thoughts, emotions, and behaviors. This quality allows you to respond more effectively to daily challenges without getting stuck in rigid or destructive thinking patterns.

Being psychologically flexible means having the capacity to embrace your internal experiences, even the difficult ones, without trying to avoid or fight them. This doesn't mean resigning yourself to suffering or passively accepting everything that happens. Rather, it's about accepting what you cannot change while focusing on what you can influence. In other words, psychological flexibility enables you to live a fuller and more satisfying life by acting in line with your values, even when the road is tough.

The importance of psychological flexibility for mental well-being cannot be overstated. People who develop this skill tend to manage stress better, maintain healthier relationships, and pursue their goals despite obstacles. On the other hand, psychological rigidity can lead to increased anxiety, depression, and other mental health issues, as it pushes you to react automatically and defensively to challenges.

For example, if you find yourself thinking, "I'll never be able to do this," psychological flexibility allows you to notice this thought without letting it paralyze you. Instead of being stopped by fear or insecurity, you can observe the thought for what it is—just a thought—and choose to act anyway, moving toward what's important to you. In this way, the thought doesn't become a barrier but rather a part of the landscape you navigate as you work toward your goals.

Psychological flexibility deeply influences your thoughts, emotions, and behaviors. When you're flexible, you can observe your thoughts without being overwhelmed by them, accept emotions without trying to avoid or eliminate them, and act consistently with your values, even when it's challenging. This ability helps you adapt more effectively to life's changing circumstances, recover more quickly from difficult moments, and stay committed to what matters most to you.

Cultivating psychological flexibility requires practice and awareness. Through the techniques offered by ACT, such as acceptance, cognitive defusion, and committed action, you can develop greater resilience and the ability to respond more adaptively to life's challenges. Psychological flexibility is not just a strategy for handling tough times; it's a life skill that helps you navigate the complexities of existence with greater calm and determination.

Exercise 1: Exploring the Six ACT Processes

For each of the six core processes of ACT, write a brief example of how you could apply it in your daily life.

Acceptance:

_____

_____

Cognitive Defusion:

_____

_____

Self as Context:

_____

_____

Present Moment Awareness:

_____

_____

Values:

_____

_____

Committed Action:

_____

_____

Exercise 2: Assessing Psychological Flexibility

Reflect on a recent challenging situation. Describe how you responded and rate your psychological flexibility in that situation on a scale from 1 to 10.

_____

_____

_____

_____

Rate your psychological flexibility (1-10): 1 | 2 | 3 | 4 | 5 | 6 | 7 | 8 | 9 | 10

Reflection:

_____

_____

_____

Exercise 3: My Values vs. Goals

List three values that are important to you, and for each one, write a concrete goal that reflects that value.

Value	Goal

Chapter 20:

Cognitive Defusion

"The mind is a wonderful servant, but a terrible master." - Robin Sharma

In this chapter, you will discover how thoughts can trap you and limit your freedom of action. You will learn to recognize cognitive fusion in your daily life and understand how it influences your behavior. I will introduce you to various defusion techniques that you can experiment with to free yourself from the tyranny of negative thoughts. Finally, you will explore the power of language and metaphors in the defusion process. Get ready to see your thoughts from an entirely new perspective.

Understanding Cognitive Fusion

Cognitive fusion is something you experience every day, often without even realizing it. It happens when you identify so closely with your thoughts that you take them as absolute truths. It's like seeing the world through tinted lenses without realizing you're wearing glasses that distort reality.

In Acceptance and Commitment Therapy (ACT), cognitive fusion occurs when you treat your thoughts as unquestionable facts instead of recognizing them for what they are: temporary mental events. Essentially, you cling to your thoughts as if they were concrete realities, allowing them to dictate your actions and emotions in ways that can be limiting.

This fusion drastically reduces your psychological flexibility. It prevents you from seeing alternatives, adapting to new situations, and acting in line with your deepest values. It's as if your thoughts become invisible chains that keep you bound, limiting your movements and choices.

For example, imagine you think, "I'm not good enough." When you are fused with this thought, you treat it as an absolute truth. As a result, you might avoid new challenges, pass up opportunities, or sabotage your relationships. The thought becomes a self-fulfilling prophecy, influencing your behavior in ways that confirm that belief.

Cognitive fusion shows up in many areas of daily life. Here are some common examples:

- Ruminating: You find yourself stuck in a loop of negative thoughts about a past or future event, unable to break free. It's like running on a never-ending wheel, replaying the same thoughts that keep you from living in the present.

- Constant Self-Criticism: A persistent inner voice continuously criticizes you, eroding your self-esteem and influencing every decision. This is the voice that says, "You're not enough" or "You'll never make it," making you doubt yourself at every turn.

- Excessive Worry: You constantly worry about the future, treating worst-case scenarios as if they are already happening. This leads you to live in a state of anxiety, anticipating problems that may never come.

- Rigid Labeling: You define yourself or others with labels based on single events or characteristics, like "I'm a failure" or "They're a bad person." These labels become a cage, limiting how you see yourself and others.

- Overgeneralization: A single negative event becomes a universal rule in your mind, like "I failed this task, so I'll always fail." This kind of thinking distorts your view of the world, leading you to make broad conclusions based on just a few experiences.

- Black-and-White Thinking: You see situations only in terms of black or white, without recognizing any shades of gray or intermediate possibilities. For example, if something doesn't go perfectly, you might think, "It's a total disaster," ignoring everything that went well.

- Mind Reading: You believe you know what others are thinking without any concrete evidence, acting as if those assumptions are facts. This can lead you to overreact or avoid situations based on misinterpretations.

Cognitive fusion is particularly insidious because it often happens automatically and unconsciously. You find yourself reacting to your thoughts as if they were real threats or undeniable truths, without stopping to consider alternatives or question their validity. But by recognizing these patterns and learning to distance yourself from your thoughts, you can begin to break these invisible chains and live with greater freedom and flexibility.

The Impact of Cognitive Fusion on Behavior

Cognitive fusion has a profound influence on our actions and decisions. When you are fused with your thoughts, you tend to react to them as if they were absolute truths, guiding your behavior in ways that are often rigid and inflexible. This can lead to a pattern of avoidance, where you steer clear of situations that trigger uncomfortable thoughts or emotions.

How Cognitive Fusion Influences Our Actions and Decisions

When you believe your thoughts to be factual rather than transient mental events, you might find yourself making decisions based on these thoughts without questioning their validity. For instance, if you're fused with the thought "I'm not capable," you might avoid applying for a job promotion or taking on a new challenge. This thought becomes a barrier, dictating your choices and limiting your potential.

Cognitive fusion also leads to automatic reactions. Instead of responding to situations with awareness and choice, you might react impulsively based on the thought that dominates your mind. This lack of mindful decision-making often results in behaviors that are not aligned with your true values or long-term goals.

The Role of Cognitive Fusion in Experiential Avoidance

Experiential avoidance is a common outcome of cognitive fusion. When you are overly identified with your thoughts, especially negative ones, you might go to great lengths to avoid experiences that could trigger those thoughts. For example, if you are fused with the thought "I can't handle failure," you might avoid taking any risks that could lead to failure, even if they align with your values or goals.

This avoidance can manifest in various forms, such as procrastination, social withdrawal, or substance abuse. By trying to avoid discomfort, you inadvertently reinforce the power of those thoughts, making them even more influential in guiding your behavior.

Long-Term Consequences of Cognitive Fusion

Over time, the impact of cognitive fusion on your behavior can lead to significant negative consequences. Persistent avoidance of challenging situations can result in missed opportunities for growth and learning. It can also reinforce a cycle of negative thinking, where each avoidance behavior confirms the validity of the original thought, making it even harder to break free from this pattern.

Additionally, cognitive fusion can contribute to chronic stress and anxiety. Constantly reacting to your thoughts as if they were threats can keep your mind and body in a heightened state of alertness, leading to physical and mental health issues over time.

In relationships, cognitive fusion can lead to misunderstandings and conflicts. When you are fused with thoughts like "They don't care about me" or "I'm not good enough," you may interpret others' actions through these distorted lenses, leading to unnecessary tension and distance.

Breaking free from cognitive fusion requires developing the ability to observe your thoughts without being controlled by them. By cultivating this skill, you can create more space for flexibility in your behavior, making choices that are aligned with your values rather than dictated by fleeting mental events. This shift can lead to a more fulfilling and balanced life, where you are guided by what truly matters to you, rather than by the automatic thoughts that arise in your mind.

Cognitive Defusion

Cognitive defusion is about changing the way you interact with your thoughts. Instead of getting caught up in them, you learn to observe them from a distance, reducing their impact on your emotions and behavior. Below are various cognitive defusion techniques you can experiment with, each designed to help you develop a new relationship with your thoughts.

- Labeling Thoughts: One of the simplest techniques is to label your thoughts for what they are. When a thought arises, say to yourself, "I'm having the thought that..." For example, instead of thinking, "I'm a failure," you might say, "I'm having the thought that I'm a failure." This labeling helps you recognize that the thought is just a product of your mind, not an absolute truth.

- Singing Thoughts: This technique involves taking a negative thought and singing it to a familiar tune. Imagine singing "I'm not good enough" as if it were the chorus of a pop song. By doing this, the thought becomes less threatening and serious, helping to reduce its emotional impact and make it easier to handle.

- Repeating Thoughts: Another effective technique is to repeat a thought over and over again, slowly, until it loses its emotional significance. For example, if you keep saying "I can't do this" repeatedly, the thought may start to seem like just a string of words with no real power over you. This repetition can strip the thought of its emotional charge, making it easier to let go.

- Imagining Thoughts on Leaves in a Stream: In this visualization technique, you imagine your thoughts written on leaves floating down a stream. Each time a thought arises, place it on a leaf and watch it drift away. This exercise helps you see thoughts as temporary and moving, rather than fixed and permanent, allowing you to let them go more easily.

- Putting Thoughts on a Cloud: Similar to the leaves technique, you can imagine your thoughts written on a cloud that slowly drifts away in the sky. This helps you distance yourself from the thought and view it from a broader perspective, seeing it as just one part of the passing scenery of your mind.

- Silly Voices: Take a troubling thought and say it out loud in a silly voice, like that of a cartoon character. For example, imagine saying "I'll never succeed" in a high-pitched, squeaky voice. This technique diminishes the seriousness of the thought and helps you see it as less threatening.

- Thought Watching: Imagine yourself sitting by a river, observing your thoughts as if they were floating by on the water. Don't try to stop them or push them away; just watch them pass. This exercise encourages you to observe your thoughts without getting entangled in them, fostering a sense of detachment.

Selecting the right defusion technique is a personal journey, and it's important to find methods that resonate with you. Start by experimenting with different techniques to see which ones feel most natural. You might find that certain approaches, like labeling thoughts or visualizing them on leaves, are easier to integrate into your daily life.

Consider the context in which you're applying these techniques. For example, if you frequently experience intrusive thoughts at work, a quick mental labeling technique might be more practical than a longer visualization exercise. At home, however, you might have more time to engage in detailed imagery, such as placing thoughts on clouds or leaves.

You might also find that combining techniques enhances their effectiveness. For instance, you could start by labeling a thought and then imagine it drifting away on a cloud. This layering of methods can reinforce the defusion process, especially when dealing with persistent or challenging thoughts.

Regular practice is key to mastering these techniques. The more you use them, the more naturally they'll come to you when you need them most. Over time, you'll develop the ability to observe your thoughts with greater detachment, allowing you to make choices that better align with your values and goals.

Common Metaphors for Defusion

In Acceptance and Commitment Therapy (ACT), metaphors are used to help you see thoughts for what they are: simply mental events, not absolute truths. Here are some of the most common metaphors for practicing defusion:

- Leaves on a Stream: Imagine sitting beside a stream, watching leaves floating on the water. Each leaf represents a thought. The stream carries them away slowly, and you don't have to do anything to change or stop the thoughts. You just observe them as they pass by and let them go.

- Passing Clouds: Thoughts are likened to clouds moving across the sky. You can't control the movement of the clouds, but you can watch them pass by. Similarly, you can allow thoughts to come and go without holding onto them, recognizing that they are only temporary.

- Racing Train: Imagine your thoughts as cars on a train speeding past you. You can choose to board the train and be carried away, or you can stay on the platform and watch the train go by without getting involved. This metaphor helps you visualize the choice not to be swept away by your thoughts, maintaining emotional distance.

- Movie Theater: Visualize yourself sitting in a movie theater, watching a screen where your thoughts are playing out. You are the spectator, not the main character in the film. You can watch the thoughts without getting caught up in their storyline, recognizing that they are not reality, but simply images projected by your mind.

- Mind Garden: Imagine your mind as a garden and your thoughts as seeds falling into it. Some seeds grow into weeds, others into flowers. You can't control which seeds arrive, but you can decide how to manage what grows in your garden. This metaphor helps you recognize that you can choose which thoughts to nurture and which to let go.

- Cars in Traffic: Think of your thoughts as cars passing by while you stand on the side of the road. You don't have to chase every car that passes; you can just let them drive on. This image helps to separate your identity from your thoughts, showing that you can observe them without having to follow them.

- Radio Noise: Imagine having a radio on in the background, playing songs or news that don't interest you. You can acknowledge it as just background noise, something you don't need to listen to or take seriously. This metaphor helps you see unwanted thoughts as mere mental noise, without real power.

- The Chessboard: Imagine your mind as a chessboard, where each piece represents a thought or emotion. The black pieces may be negative thoughts, and the white pieces may be positive ones. Instead of being one of the pieces caught up in the game, you are the chessboard itself. This metaphor helps you understand that you are the context in which thoughts occur, not the thoughts themselves.

- The Bus Driver: Picture yourself as the driver of a bus, with your thoughts and emotions as passengers. Some passengers are loud and demanding, others are quiet, but you remain in control of where the bus goes. You acknowledge the passengers, but you don't let them dictate your route. This metaphor emphasizes your ability to take action based on your values, despite the noise of your thoughts.

- The Sky and the Weather: Think of your mind as the sky, and your thoughts and emotions as different weather patterns. Sometimes it's sunny (positive thoughts), and other times it's stormy (negative thoughts), but the sky remains unchanged and vast, no matter what weather passes through it. This metaphor illustrates that your true self is constant and unaffected by temporary thoughts.

- Sticky Notes: Imagine each of your thoughts is written on a sticky note that you've stuck to your face. These notes obscure your vision and make it hard to see the world clearly. By peeling off each note and holding it at arm's length, you can see it for what it is—just a thought—allowing you to regain perspective and clarity.

- The Thought Train: Visualize your thoughts as a series of train cars passing by on a track. You can decide whether to jump on the train and be carried away by your thoughts, or you can stand on the platform and watch the train go by. This metaphor helps you practice choosing not to engage with certain thoughts.

- Monsters on a Boat: Picture yourself on a boat, with various monsters (representing your fears and unwanted thoughts) surrounding it. As long as you stay focused on where you want to go, the monsters can't harm you. This metaphor illustrates that while your thoughts and fears may always be present, they don't have to control your direction in life.

- Balloons in the Sky: Imagine your thoughts as balloons that you're holding onto. Each thought is attached to a string that you can choose to hold tightly or let go. As you release each balloon, it drifts away into the sky, allowing you to focus on the present moment. This metaphor helps you practice letting go of unhelpful thoughts.

- The Audience in a Theater: Picture yourself on stage, with your thoughts and emotions as the audience. Some members of the audience are supportive, while others are critical. Instead of trying to control the audience, focus on your performance and what you want to achieve on stage. This metaphor emphasizes the importance of focusing on your values and actions, rather than trying to control or appease your thoughts.

These metaphors create psychological distance between you and your thoughts, allowing you to see them as mental events rather than absolute realities. By using these metaphors regularly, you can improve your ability to manage negative or intrusive thoughts, enhancing your psychological flexibility.

Creating Personal Metaphors

While common metaphors can be incredibly useful, creating your own personal metaphors can make them even more powerful and relevant to your individual experience. The key is to find images or scenarios that resonate with you and represent how you want to relate to your thoughts.

To start crafting personal metaphors, reflect on experiences or activities that are familiar to you. For example, if you love gardening, you might imagine your thoughts as weeds in the garden of your mind. You can't stop them from growing, but you can choose not to let them take over the garden. You can simply observe them sprout and then decide if and when to pull them out.

If you're passionate about sports, you might compare your thoughts to a stopwatch ticking away in the background during a game. The stopwatch is there, but you don't need to focus on it; you can choose to concentrate on the game and let the ticking continue without interfering with your performance.

Personal metaphors work best when they reflect your interests and daily experiences. This makes them easier to remember and apply when needed. Additionally, because they are created by you, these metaphors can evolve with you, adapting to changes in your circumstances or perspectives.

When using these metaphors, remember that the goal isn't to eliminate or change your thoughts, but to change the way you relate to them. Metaphors give you a way to step back from your thoughts, allowing you to see them for what they are: mere products of the mind, without any real control over your life unless you let them.

Consider experimenting with different metaphors and tweaking them until you find the ones that work best for you. You might even combine multiple metaphors to address different situations or to respond to specific types of thoughts. Over time and with practice, these mental images will become valuable tools for maintaining a healthy distance from your thoughts, enhancing your ability to live more freely and authentically.

Exercise 1: Thought Observer

For 5 minutes, observe your thoughts as if they were clouds in the sky. Write down the thoughts you notice without judging or trying to change them.

Thoughts observed:

1. _____

2. _____

3. _____

4. _____

5. _____

Reflection on the experience:

_____

_____

_____

_____

_____

_____

Exercise 2: Labeling Thoughts

Identify three recurring thoughts that cause you discomfort. For each one, create a neutral label. The goal is to step back and simply acknowledge the thought as a mental event, rather than something that defines you.

Example: Original thought: "I always mess things up." Label created: "Here's the thought that I'm not capable."

Original Thought	Label Created
"I always mess things up."	*"Here's the thought that I'm not capable."*

Exercise 3: Personal Defusion Metaphor

Create a personal metaphor to describe the process of defusion. Then, explain how you might use this metaphor when you feel fused with your thoughts.

My defusion metaphor:

_____

_____

_____

How I will use this metaphor:

_____

_____

_____

Chapter 21:

Self as Context

"I am not what happened to me, I am what I choose to become." – Carl Jung

In this chapter, you will explore a fundamental concept in Acceptance and Commitment Therapy: self as context. You'll discover how this perspective can transform your relationship with thoughts and emotions, offering you new freedom in facing life's challenges. You will examine the difference between the conceptualized self and the observing self, understand the power of transcendent perspective, and learn how mindfulness intertwines with this practice.

The Conceptualized Self vs. the Observing Self

Think for a moment about how you describe yourself. You likely use adjectives like "intelligent," "anxious," "ambitious," or "shy." You may define yourself through your roles: parent, professional, friend. This is the voice of your conceptualized self—the image you've constructed of yourself over time, based on experiences, feedback from others, and personal beliefs.

The conceptualized self is like a label you've attached to yourself. Sometimes it can be helpful, guiding you through social interactions and helping you make decisions aligned with your identity. However, it can also become a cage, limiting your possibilities and influencing how you interpret experiences.

Imagine considering yourself "an anxious person." This label might lead you to avoid situations you perceive as stressful, reinforcing your belief that you are anxious. The conceptualized self can create a vicious cycle, narrowing your range of action and feeding behaviors that confirm your self-perception.

Now, imagine being able to step back and observe these thoughts and labels from a different perspective. This is the function of the observing self. The observing self is the part of you that can notice your thoughts, emotions, and sensations without being completely absorbed by them.

The observing self is like a vast and expansive sky, while your thoughts and emotions are like clouds passing through. Sometimes the clouds may be dark and threatening, other times light and fluffy, but the sky remains constant, unchanging, and capable of containing any weather condition.

This perspective offers extraordinary freedom. When you identify with the observing self, you are no longer trapped by your labels or temporary emotional states. You can notice anxiety without being "an anxious person," you can experience sadness without being "depressed."

The observing self plays a crucial role in psychological flexibility, one of the primary goals of ACT. It allows you to respond to situations more adaptively, rather than reacting automatically based on rigid self-perceptions. When you observe your thoughts and emotions without fully identifying with them, you have more room to choose your actions in alignment with your values, rather than being driven by automatic reactions.

Cultivating the observing self does not mean denying or suppressing the conceptualized self. It's about broadening your perspective, adding a dimension of awareness that allows you to navigate life with greater flexibility and wisdom.

In the following sections, you will explore how to develop this transcendent perspective, how mindfulness can assist you in this process, and how to practically apply self as context in your daily life. Prepare to discover a new way of relating to yourself and the world around you.

The Transcendent Perspective

The transcendent perspective is a key to living with greater inner freedom. It allows you to step back from the chaos of thoughts and emotions that sometimes seem to define you, and gives you the ability to see yourself and your experiences from a broader, more stable vantage point. Imagine having the ability to observe your life not just through your own eyes, but from a viewpoint that encompasses the entire landscape. It's as if you could rise above the noise and confusion, seeing things from a distance that makes everything a bit clearer and more manageable.

This transcendent perspective helps you recognize that your thoughts, emotions, and roles are just part of the flow of your experience. They are not your entire identity. This awareness gives you the opportunity to view everything happening inside of you with more detachment and calm, without getting stuck in it.

Often, we fully identify with our thoughts. If a negative thought arises, such as "I'm not good enough," we tend to believe that thought as if it were the absolute truth about who we are. The transcendent perspective teaches us that we are not what we think. Instead, we are the space in which thoughts arise and disappear. This space—the observing self—is vast, stable, and ever-present, even when our mind is in turmoil.

A helpful way to understand this idea is to think of your mind as the sky. Thoughts and emotions are the clouds passing through it. Some clouds are white and fluffy, others dark and stormy, but the sky remains unchanged, no matter the weather. The sky doesn't fight the clouds; it simply allows them to pass by. In the same way, you can let your thoughts and emotions move through your awareness without needing to fight them or identify with them as permanent parts of who you are.

Cultivating this perspective is not an act of denial or avoidance. It doesn't mean ignoring what you feel or think, but it means recognizing that there is a part of you that is larger than any single thought or emotion. When you step back from what your mind is telling you, you gain incredible freedom. You are no longer bound by labels like "I am an anxious person" or "I'm always insecure." You are something more—something that observes these thoughts but is not defined by them.

This may seem like an abstract concept, but it's actually very practical. For example, think of the last time you felt overwhelmed by an emotion like anger. When you're in the midst of that anger, it feels like it consumes you completely. Everything you feel and think is colored by that emotion. But if you can step back, even for a moment, and recognize that the anger is just a cloud passing through the sky of your being, you can start to see that you have a choice. You don't have to act on the anger. You can simply notice it, let it be, and then let it go when it's ready to pass.

A powerful tool for developing this transcendent perspective is mindfulness. Mindfulness helps you focus on the present moment and, perhaps more importantly, teaches you to observe what is happening without judgment. Instead of getting swept up in the whirlwind of thoughts and emotions, you begin to cultivate the ability to be present with what is happening, but with some distance. You are not your thoughts; you are the one who observes them.

An exercise that can help you develop this awareness is the "mountain meditation." Imagine yourself as a solid, grounded mountain. The weather—wind, rain, sunshine, storms—is like your thoughts and emotions. While everything around you changes, you, the mountain, remain steady. The weather comes and goes, but your essence—the mountain—stays the same. This image helps reinforce the idea that no matter what is happening in your mind, there is a part of you that is always stable and rooted.

The transcendent perspective isn't just a concept for formal meditation or reflection, but it can become a way of living each day. In moments of stress or difficulty, you can remind yourself to step back and observe. Instead of reacting automatically to your thoughts and feelings, you can give yourself space to choose how to respond. That space is your freedom. And the more you cultivate this perspective, the more natural it becomes.

The transcendent perspective teaches you that you can be present with any experience without being defined by it. You are something greater than your thoughts, larger than your emotions, and more stable than your personal stories. This awareness can transform the way you live your life, bringing you greater serenity, resilience, and inner freedom.

As you begin to live from this perspective, you discover that even in the most challenging moments, there is a part of you that remains calm and centered. And from this place of calm, you can approach any challenge with more wisdom and flexibility. You are not trapped in your reactions, but free to choose how you respond. And this, perhaps, is the true essence of psychological freedom.

Guided Meditation

The concept of self as context can be a source of great calm and stability, especially when we learn to practice it mindfully. In this section, you will explore a guided meditation designed to help you cultivate awareness of the observing self. Through this practice, you will be able to directly experience how the self as context allows you to observe thoughts, emotions, and sensations without fully identifying with them.

Step 1: Preparation

Find a quiet place where you can sit comfortably without being disturbed. You can sit on a chair with your feet flat on the ground or cross-legged on a cushion. Keep your back straight but relaxed. Gently close your eyes and take a few deep breaths, inhaling through your nose and exhaling through your mouth. Allow your body to relax, letting your shoulders drop and your jaw loosen.

Step 2: Connecting with the Body

Now, bring your attention to your body. Notice the points of contact with the floor or the chair—feel the weight of your body resting on the surface beneath you. Bring awareness to these sensations without trying to change them.

Begin a slow body scan, starting from the top of your head and moving down to your feet. Notice any tension, discomfort, or even pleasant or neutral sensations. You don't need to change what you feel, just observe with curiosity and acceptance. Recognize that these sensations are part of the present experience, but they are not all of who you are.

Step 3: Observing Thoughts

Next, gently shift your attention to the thoughts that arise. Imagine each thought is like a cloud passing through the sky of your mind. It could be random thoughts, worries, memories, or plans for the future. Whatever arises, simply observe it without trying to hold on to it or push it away.

Notice each thought as it appears and mentally repeat to yourself: "This is just a thought, it is not who I am." Let the thought pass as it came, knowing that you are something greater than your thoughts—you are the space in which they appear.

Step 4: Observing Emotions

Now, bring your attention to any emotions that may be present. What emotions are you feeling right now? You might notice feelings of joy, anxiety, calm, or restlessness. Observe these emotions as if they were temporary visitors.

If you feel a particularly strong emotion, simply acknowledge it by saying to yourself: "I am noticing [name of the emotion]." Then, remind yourself that this emotion is just part of your experience. You can notice it without being defined by it. Like a cloud in the sky, this emotion is a temporary experience.

Step 5: Expanding Awareness

Now, visualize the self as a vast, open, and stable space, like a clear and infinite sky. Your thoughts and emotions are clouds passing through this sky. Some clouds may be dark and threatening, while others are light and serene, but the sky remains the same—wide, calm, and able to contain everything that happens.

As you practice this visualization, cultivate the awareness that you are this vast and open sky. You are the context, not the content of your experiences. Both thoughts and emotions pass through, but you, the sky, remain stable and unchanging.

Step 6: Grounding in the Self as Context

Acknowledge that while thoughts and emotions move and change, you are always the space that holds them. You are the silent observer, the witness to your experiences. This awareness of the observing self is always available to you, even in moments of difficulty or stress. You can always return to this space of calm and observation.

Allow yourself to rest in this awareness for a few minutes, knowing that even when everything around you seems to change, there is a part of you that remains stable and grounded.

Step 7: Closing the Meditation

When you are ready, begin to slowly bring your attention back to your body. Notice again the points of contact with the floor or chair, and gently start to move your fingers and toes. Breathe deeply for a few moments, maintaining the awareness of the self as context.

When you feel ready, slowly open your eyes. Take a moment to notice how you feel physically and emotionally compared to before the meditation. Carry this awareness of the observing self with you for the rest of your day, remembering that you can always return to this perspective of calm and stability.

Exercise 1: Observer Exercise

Close your eyes and spend a few minutes observing your thoughts, feelings, and bodily sensations. Then, write down what you noticed, emphasizing your ability to observe these experiences.

Observations:

_____

_____

_____

Reflection on the observation experience:

_____

_____

_____

Exercise 2: I Notice

Complete 10 sentences that begin with "I notice...", focusing on your current thoughts, feelings, or sensations.

1. I notice ...
_____

2.
_____

3.
_____

4.
_____

5.
_____

6.
_____

7.
_____

8.
_____

9.
_____

10.
_____

Exercise 3: Letter from the Observing Self

Write a brief letter to yourself from the perspective of your observing self, offering wisdom and compassion regarding a difficult situation you are facing.

Dear

_____

_____

_____

_____

_____

_____

_____

_____

_____

_____

_____

_____

_____

_____

_____

_____

_____

_____

With compassion and wisdom,
Your Observing Self

Chapter 22:

Acceptance and Willingness

"The curious paradox is that when I accept myself just as I am, then I can change." - Carl Rogers

In this chapter, we will explore two fundamental concepts of ACT: acceptance and willingness. You will discover how these processes can transform your relationship with difficult thoughts and emotions, paving the way for a richer, more meaningful life.

The Difference Between Acceptance and Resignation

Acceptance is often misunderstood. Many confuse it with resignation or passive tolerance of unpleasant situations. However, in ACT, acceptance takes on a very different and far more powerful meaning.

Acceptance is an active process of opening up to the present experience without trying to change or escape it. It involves embracing thoughts, emotions, and sensations as they arise, without judging or attempting to suppress them. This attitude doesn't mean you have to like what you're experiencing, but rather that you are willing to fully experience it.

Resignation, on the other hand, involves a kind of passive surrender. When you resign, you give up any possibility of change and yield to the circumstances. ACT-style acceptance is the exact opposite: it is an active step towards a richer and more meaningful life.

Imagine standing in front of a brick wall. Resignation would be like sitting down in front of the wall, convinced there's no way to get past it. Acceptance, however, means acknowledging the wall's presence, observing it carefully, and then deciding how to act: whether to climb over it, find a way around it, or perhaps even use it as support to reach something higher.

Passive tolerance is another concept that differs from acceptance. Tolerating something means enduring something unpleasant, often while waiting for it to pass. ACT's acceptance, however, invites you to make direct contact with the experience, to explore it with curiosity, without passively waiting for it to fade away.

Acceptance plays a crucial role in psychological flexibility, one of the main goals of ACT. When you accept your thoughts and emotions, you create the mental space necessary to respond flexibly to situations, rather than automatically reacting based on old patterns. This doesn't mean that negative thoughts or difficult emotions will disappear, but their impact on your life will lessen.

By practicing acceptance, you may discover that some experiences you once thought were unbearable are actually manageable. This not only reduces your suffering but also allows you to invest more energy in the things that truly matter to you. In this way, acceptance becomes a springboard for change, not an obstacle.

Remember: acceptance does not mean giving up or stopping the desire for a better life. Rather, it is a way to create the necessary conditions for change, starting from where you are right now. By accepting what is present, you free up mental and emotional resources that can then be used to move in the direction of your values.

In the next section, we will examine how attempts to control difficult experiences can paradoxically increase psychological distress and how ACT's approach offers a more effective alternative.

The Role of Control in Psychological Distress

Control is often seen as the key to managing our internal experiences. We believe that if we can control our thoughts and emotions, we can avoid distress and live peacefully. This belief forms the basis of what, in ACT, we call the "control agenda."

The control agenda is the often unconscious strategy we adopt to try to eliminate or change unpleasant internal experiences. It can manifest in various ways: trying to suppress negative thoughts, distracting ourselves from painful emotions, or avoiding situations that might trigger anxiety. At first glance, these strategies might seem logical. After all, who wouldn't want to get rid of discomfort?

The problem is that the control agenda has significant limitations. First and foremost, it rarely works in the long run. Try not to think of a pink elephant. What happens? Chances are, the image of a pink elephant immediately popped into your mind. This simple experiment demonstrates how attempting to control your thoughts can have the opposite effect.

The same principle applies to emotions. When you try not to feel anxious, you often end up focusing even more on the anxiety, intensifying it. It's like trying not to think of the pink elephant: the more you try, the harder it becomes.

But there's more. The constant effort to control can actually increase psychological distress in several ways:

- Hypervigilance: You find yourself constantly on alert, searching for thoughts or emotions to control. This ongoing tension becomes a source of stress in itself.

- Rebound Effect: When you try to suppress a thought or emotion, it often returns with greater intensity once control is relaxed.

- Experiential Avoidance: By avoiding situations that might trigger discomfort, you limit your life experiences and opportunities for growth.

- Sense of Failure: When control efforts don't work, you may feel frustrated and inadequate, further feeding the distress.

- Distraction from Meaningful Activities: The energy spent on trying to control takes you away from what truly matters to you.

Imagine being caught in a river's current. Fighting against the current (the attempt to control) exhausts you and often carries you further away from where you want to go. The alternative proposed by ACT is more like allowing yourself to be carried by the current, observing the changing landscape (willingness), while using your energy to steer toward your desired direction.

Willingness, a key concept in ACT, is the alternative to control. It is an attitude of openness toward internal experiences, regardless of whether they are pleasant or unpleasant. It doesn't mean you like difficult experiences, but rather that you are willing to let them exist without fighting against them.

Practicing willingness involves:

- Observing your internal experiences without judgment.

- Accepting that thoughts and emotions come and go naturally.

- Recognizing that you can have a thought or emotion without being defined by it.

- Allowing difficult experiences to exist while moving toward what matters to you.

Willingness is not passive resignation. On the contrary, it is an active way of relating to your experiences that frees up energy and attention. Instead of wasting resources trying to control the uncontrollable, you can invest them in actions aligned with your values.

Adopting an attitude of willingness requires practice and patience. At first, it may feel counterintuitive or even frightening. However, over time, many people find that this approach leads to greater psychological freedom and a more meaningful life.

Developing Emotional Willingness

Emotional willingness is the ability to remain open and receptive to your inner experiences, whether they are pleasant or unpleasant. It doesn't mean liking or wanting negative emotions, but rather creating space for all emotions to exist without the need to fight them or be overwhelmed by them.

Imagine your mind as a vast sky. Emotions and thoughts are like clouds passing through: some are dark and threatening, others light and bright. Emotional willingness allows you to observe these clouds without trying to dispel or cling to them, recognizing that, like the sky, you are larger and more enduring than any passing cloud.

Here are some effective techniques to increase your willingness to face difficult experiences:

- Mindful Observation:

  Spend a few minutes each day observing your emotions without judging them. Notice where you feel them in your body, how their intensity changes, and how they move. This detached observation can help you see emotions as temporary events rather than absolute truths about yourself or the world.

- Passenger on the Bus Metaphor:

  Imagine you are the driver of a bus. Your thoughts and emotions are passengers who get on and off. Some are noisy and irritating, others quiet and pleasant. Your job is not to make the unpleasant passengers get off, but to keep driving the bus in the direction you've chosen, regardless of who is on board.

- Expansion Exercise:

  When you experience a difficult emotion, instead of contracting around it, try to "expand" around it. Imagine creating space within yourself to accommodate that emotion, allowing it to exist without trying to change it.

- Paradoxical Gratitude Practice:

  Try to find a reason to be grateful, even for difficult experiences. For example, anxiety before an exam might indicate that you care about your performance. This doesn't mean you have to love the anxiety, but you can recognize that it might have a role in your life.

- The "And" Technique:

  When you find yourself in a difficult situation, use the conjunction "and" instead of "but." For example, instead of thinking, "I'm anxious, but I have to stay calm," try, "I'm anxious, and I choose to move forward with my goals." This allows you to accept the emotion without denying or fighting against it.

Developing emotional willingness requires practice and patience. At first, you may find it challenging to remain open to intense or unpleasant emotions. That's normal. Remember, the goal isn't to eliminate discomfort but to learn how to live with it more flexibly.

Emotional willingness isn't an end in itself, but it supports and integrates with other key ACT processes:

- Cognitive Defusion:

  Willingness helps you create space between yourself and your thoughts, facilitating the process of defusion. When you are willing to accept even unpleasant thoughts, it becomes easier to see them as mere mental events rather than absolute truths.

- Present-Moment Awareness:

  Being willing to experience your emotions naturally anchors you in the here and now. Instead of getting lost in future worries or past regrets, willingness encourages you to stay present with what is happening at this moment.

- Self as Context:

  The practice of willingness strengthens your ability to observe your experiences from a broader perspective. This supports the development of the "observing self," a part of you that can notice thoughts and emotions without being defined by them.

- Values:
  Being willing to face difficult emotions allows you to act in line with your values even when circumstances aren't ideal. For example, you might choose to speak in public despite feeling anxious if it aligns with your value of sharing knowledge.

- Committed Action:

  Emotional willingness gives you the flexibility needed to take meaningful action even in the presence of internal obstacles. Instead of waiting to feel "ready" or "motivated," you can move toward your goals while bringing along whatever emotions arise.

In the next section, we will explore how acceptance can paradoxically become a powerful catalyst for change in your life.

Acceptance as a Path to Change

The paradox of acceptance and change is one of the most fascinating and counterintuitive concepts in ACT. At first glance, it might seem that accepting something means resigning and giving up on change. In reality, acceptance often becomes the most powerful catalyst for authentic and lasting transformation.

This paradox reveals itself when you realize that struggling against your current reality drains precious energy that could instead be invested in change. By accepting what is, you free up mental and emotional resources to move toward what you want it to be.

Imagine being stuck in quicksand. The more you struggle and fight, the deeper you sink. Acceptance is like stopping the struggle: it doesn't immediately pull you out, but it gives you the calm needed to think clearly and find a solution.

Acceptance facilitates behavioral change in several ways:

- Reduces Avoidance:

  When you accept difficult thoughts and emotions, you are less likely to avoid situations that might trigger them. This allows you to face challenges you might have previously evaded, opening up new opportunities for growth.

- Increases Awareness:

  By accepting your internal experiences, you become more aware of your thought and behavior patterns. This heightened self-awareness is the first step toward intentional change.

- Frees Up Energy:

  Constantly battling unwanted thoughts and emotions consumes a lot of mental energy. Acceptance frees this energy, allowing you to focus on constructive actions.

- Promotes Flexibility:

  Accepting that your internal experiences can vary makes you more flexible in how you respond to situations. You are no longer "held hostage" by a particular mood in order to act.

- Reduces Self-Criticism:

  Self-acceptance decreases the tendency for destructive self-criticism, which often hinders change more than it promotes it.

Integrating acceptance with committed action is key to achieving meaningful change. Committed action involves taking concrete steps toward your goals, aligned with your values, regardless of how you feel in the moment.

Here's how you can integrate acceptance and committed action:

1. Recognize and accept your current thoughts and emotions.

2. Connect with your values: What is truly important to you in this situation?

3. Identify an action, even a small one, that moves you closer to your goals.

4. Act, carrying along any thoughts or emotions that arise.

5. Reflect on the experience, accepting both the successes and the difficulties encountered.

For example, if you want to improve your social relationships but struggle with social anxiety, you might:

1. Accept the anxious thoughts and physical sensations that arise.

2. Reconnect with your value of human connection.

3. Decide to send a message to a friend to arrange a meeting.

4. Send the message, welcoming the anxiety that may emerge.

5. Reflect on the experience, accepting both the satisfaction of taking action and any discomfort you felt.

Acceptance is not an end, but a means. You do not accept in order to resign yourself but to create the space necessary for change. It's like taking a step back to gain momentum: sometimes, to move forward, we first need to accept where we are.

By practicing the integration of acceptance and committed action, you'll discover that change doesn't require you to always feel good or motivated. You can progress toward your goals while carrying the full range of your human experiences, accepting them as part of the journey.

Exercise 1: Acceptance Journal

For 5 days, identify a situation in which you practiced acceptance. Describe the situation, what you accepted, and how you felt afterward.

Day	Situation	What I Accepted	How I Felt Afterward
	I had a disagreement with a colleague at work.	*I accepted my feelings of frustration and disappointment, instead of trying to suppress them.*	*I felt more at peace because I allowed myself to feel frustrated without judgment, and I was able to respond calmly.*

Exercise 2: Willingness Exercise

Think about an emotion or sensation that you often try to avoid. Write about how you might practice willingness toward this experience.

Emotion or sensation I try to avoid:

How I might practice willingness toward this experience:

_____

_____

_____

_____

_____

_____

Exercise 3: Personal Acceptance Metaphor

Create a personal metaphor to describe acceptance. Then, explain how this metaphor might help you during difficult times.

My metaphor for acceptance:

_____

_____

_____

How I would use this metaphor in difficult times:

_____

_____

_____

_____

_____

Chapter 23:

Values

"Values are like fingerprints. Nobody's are the same, but you leave 'em all over everything you do." - Elvis Presley

This chapter focuses on the role values play in your life. Values represent what truly matters to you and influence every aspect of your existence. They are the principles that inspire and guide you over the long term. Unlike goals, which are concrete and measurable milestones, values don't have an endpoint. They are ongoing guidelines that shape your choices and the way you approach different situations in life.

Defining your values means taking time to reflect deeply on what is truly important to you. These might be related to personal growth, honesty, meaningful relationships, health, or creativity. It's important that these values come from within you, not from others' expectations. When you have clarity about what matters, you can make more conscious decisions that are in line with who you are.

A key difference between values and goals is that, unlike goals, values cannot be "achieved." Goals are completed, while values remain constant over time. For example, you may set the goal of completing a marathon, but the value driving you could be respect for your health or discipline. Even after finishing the marathon, that value will continue to influence your behavior in other areas of your life, such as maintaining a healthy diet or regular exercise.

Values play a crucial role in promoting psychological flexibility. Having clarity about your values allows you to face changes and challenges with greater calm, while still maintaining a strong sense of direction. This way, even when you encounter difficulties, you can stay grounded in your convictions and choose actions that reflect what truly matters to you. Values become a constant reference point, helping you navigate even the most uncertain or stressful situations.

Identifying Personal Values

Identifying your personal values is a crucial step in living authentically and in alignment with what truly matters to you. However, discovering your core values requires introspection and self-awareness. This process can be complex, as we often confuse our true values with those imposed by external influences like family, society, or culture.

There are several techniques that can help you identify your personal values. Here are some of the most effective ones:

- Reflecting on Significant Experiences

  A great place to start is by reflecting on the most meaningful experiences in your life. What events made you feel deeply fulfilled or, on the contrary, left you feeling disappointed? Analyzing these situations helps you uncover the principles that made them significant. For example, if you felt a strong sense of satisfaction when helping someone in need, you might discover that compassion or altruism is one of your core values.

- Visualizing the Future

  Another helpful technique is to imagine yourself in the future, looking back on your life. What do you want to remember with pride? What qualities or behaviors would you like to have characterized your journey? This exercise helps you identify the values you wish to embody and that represent the kind of person you want to be.

- Values Questionnaires

  There are many questionnaires and tools available to help you explore your values. These tools ask targeted questions that encourage you to reflect on what motivates you and what your priorities are. While these questionnaires don't provide definitive answers, they offer valuable insights into your values and spark further reflection.

- Exploring Intense Emotions

  Another way to discover your values is by exploring the intense emotions you feel in different situations. Emotions, whether positive or negative, often signal your values. Anger or frustration may reveal violated values, while joy or satisfaction can indicate when your values have been honored. Take some time to analyze these emotions and ask yourself which principles underlie your emotional reactions.

Values manifest in various aspects of your life. For a more comprehensive understanding of what truly matters to you, it can be helpful to explore the different domains of your existence. Here are some of the key areas:

- Relationships: Your interactions with friends, family, and partners are guided by the values you attach to relationships. You might discover that loyalty, trust, or empathy are central values for you in this domain. Reflecting on what makes your relationships meaningful helps clarify these values.

- Career: In the professional context, values may relate to integrity, innovation, creativity, or commitment. Think about what drives you to do your best work and what gives you a sense of fulfillment. This will help you identify the values that guide your professional decisions.

- Personal Growth: In this area, values may include the pursuit of knowledge, wisdom, authenticity, or continuous improvement. Reflect on what motivates you to grow and evolve as a person.

- Health and Well-Being: Your personal care and physical and emotional well-being are also influenced by your values. Health, balance, and resilience might be key principles for you in this area.

- Leisure and Creativity: The activities you choose to engage in during your free time reflect what you are passionate about and what regenerates you. You might find that values such as freedom, adventure, or creativity are essential to your well-being.

Analyzing these life domains helps you recognize how values can vary across different contexts, while also identifying the principles that remain constant and permeate every aspect of your existence.

Recognizing Authentic Values vs. Externally Imposed Values

Distinguishing between authentic values and those imposed from outside is crucial for living a fulfilling and meaningful life. Often, the values we follow aren't truly our own, but are instead shaped by family, societal, or cultural pressures. For instance, you might believe that financial success is an important value, but only because your family or society led you to think so. However, this may not be what genuinely brings you inner fulfillment.

To recognize authentic values, you need to step back and reflect on whether the principles you follow are truly yours or have been imposed. Here are some tips for distinguishing between authentic and imposed values:

- Listen to Your Body and Emotions: Authentic values make you feel in harmony with yourself. If a value imposed from outside makes you feel pressured, anxious, or dissatisfied, it may not be truly yours. In contrast, authentic values often bring a sense of peace and congruence.

- Ask Yourself "Why": When identifying a value, ask yourself why it is important to you. If the answer is based on external expectations or fear of judgment, it may be an imposed value. If, however, you feel that the value deeply reflects who you are and what you desire, it's likely authentic.

- Observe Your Behavior: Authentic values are reflected in your actions, even when you're not obligated to follow a certain path. If you continue to pursue something without external pressure, it's likely that the value is truly important to you.

- Be Honest with Yourself: The key to identifying your authentic values is being honest with yourself. This requires courage, as it may mean questioning beliefs you've held for years. However, this discovery process will allow you to live more in alignment with who you truly are.

Identifying your personal values gives you a solid foundation for making more intentional and mindful choices. When you live in alignment with your authentic values, every action you take carries a deeper sense of meaning and purpose, regardless of the outcome.

Aligning Actions with Values

Living in alignment with your values is one of the most significant and rewarding challenges you can undertake. It requires intentionality and commitment, but when you succeed, you create a more authentic and fulfilling life where your daily choices reflect what truly matters to you.

Strategies for Living Consistently with Your Values

- Set Clear Intentions

  The first step in living in alignment with your values is to set clear intentions. Once you have identified the values that guide your life, define specific actions that can express those values in your daily routine. For example, if one of your core values is connection with others, you might decide to spend time each day calling or meeting with someone you care about.

- Plan and Create Concrete Goals

  Defining concrete goals is a great way to turn values into action. Make sure these goals are realistic and manageable so that you can integrate them into your life without feeling overwhelmed. Goals should be specific, measurable, and directly linked to your core values. For example, if personal growth is a value for you, you might set a goal to read a certain number of books each year or to attend a training course.

- Monitor and Adjust Your Actions

  Living consistently with your values requires regular monitoring and adjustments along the way. Take time to reflect periodically to evaluate whether your daily actions are truly aligned with your values. This practice of self-reflection allows you to recognize any deviations and correct your course, keeping the focus on what is truly important to you.

Overcoming Obstacles to Value-Based Action

It's not uncommon to encounter obstacles that prevent you from living in alignment with your values. These obstacles can manifest as fear, procrastination, or external pressures. Here are some strategies to overcome them:

- Acknowledge Your Fears

  Fear is one of the most common obstacles to value-based action. You might fear failure, rejection, or uncertainty. It's important to recognize these fears without allowing them to control your choices. ACT encourages you to make space for these emotions and move forward regardless, keeping your focus on your values.

- Tackle Procrastination

  Procrastination is another barrier that can stop you from acting in line with your values. This behavior often stems from seeking immediate comfort or avoiding discomfort. To overcome procrastination, start with small, manageable steps that require less effort, creating a steady sense of progress toward your goals.

- Manage External Pressures

  Sometimes, the expectations of others or society can conflict with your values. When faced with external pressures, it helps to remember that your values are personal and unique to you. Ask yourself if the choices you're making truly reflect what you want, or if you're acting to conform to others' expectations.

- Embrace Imperfection

  No one lives perfectly aligned with their values all the time, and that's okay. The important thing is not to get discouraged by mistakes or deviations. Every misstep is an opportunity to learn and grow, and what matters is returning consistently to the path of your values with patience and determination.

How Values Support Resilience and Long-Term Well-Being

Living consistently with your values not only allows you to feel more fulfilled but also supports your resilience and long-term well-being. Here's how:

- Increased Resilience: When your actions are guided by your values, you are better equipped to face challenges with inner strength. Values provide you with a solid emotional and mental foundation that supports you even during times of crisis or uncertainty. Knowing that you are living according to what truly matters to you gives you the motivation to keep going, even when the road is tough.

- Emotional and Psychological Well-Being: Living in alignment with your values fosters a sense of integrity and inner harmony. When your actions are consistent with your principles, you experience less internal conflict and stress from living a life that doesn't reflect who you truly are. Over time, this results in improved emotional and psychological well-being.

- Meaning and Purpose: Finally, values give a deeper meaning to your actions and your life. When your choices reflect your values, even the smallest daily gestures take on a larger significance. This sense of purpose keeps you grounded and focused on what truly matters, making your life richer and more meaningful.

Exercise 1: Exploring Your Values

Example

Life Area	Value	Why It Is Meaningful
Relationships	Connection	*Building strong and supportive relationships with loved ones is essential to my happiness and well-being. It gives me a sense of belonging and purpose.*
Career	Integrity	*I value being honest and transparent in my work. Upholding integrity allows me to feel proud of my contributions and ensures that I am doing my job ethically.*
Personal Growth	Curiosity	*Lifelong learning and personal development are important to me. Staying curious allows me to constantly evolve, discover new passions, and adapt to change.*
Health	Vitality	*Taking care of my body and mind is crucial to living a long and fulfilling life. Prioritizing vitality helps me stay energetic and resilient in the face of challenges.*
Leisure	Creativity	*Engaging in creative activities, such as painting and writing, allows me to express myself freely and experience joy outside of my daily responsibilities.*

Life Area	Value	Why It Is Meaningful
Relationships		
Career		
Personal Growth		
Health		
Leisure		

Exercise 2: Values vs. Goals

Choose three of your most important values. For each value, define a concrete goal that would help you live more fully aligned with that value.

Example

Value	Goal	How This Goal Reflects the Value
Connection	*Spend quality time with my partner every weekend*	*This goal ensures that I nurture and strengthen the bond with my partner, which is key to maintaining a meaningful relationship.*
Integrity	*Complete my work projects with full transparency*	*By maintaining honesty and openness in my professional life, I uphold my commitment to ethical behavior in the workplace.*
Curiosity	*Read one new book every month on a topic I'm unfamiliar with*	*This goal fuels my desire for lifelong learning and helps me expand my knowledge and adaptability.*

Value	Goal	How This Goal Reflects the Value

Exercise 3: Living Your Values

Identify a situation in the upcoming week where you could act according to one of your values. Describe the situation and how you plan to act in line with that value. This exercise will help you put your values into practice in daily life.

Description of the situation:

_____

_____

_____

_____

_____

Relevant value:

Action plan:

_____

_____

_____

_____

_____

_____

_____

_____

_____

_____

Chapter 24:

Committed Action

"The path to success is to take massive, determined actions." - Tony Robbins

In this chapter, we will explore the importance of translating values into concrete actions. Once you have identified what truly matters to you, the next step is to act in a way that reflects your principles. We will examine how moving from values to actions not only helps bridge the gap between intention and behavior but also integrates with other processes of the ACT model to foster a more authentic and meaningful life.

Moving from Values to Action

When it comes to living in line with your values, it's action that makes the difference. Identifying what's important is just the beginning; the real challenge is translating those values into tangible behaviors. This doesn't mean simply taking one action—it's about committing to making consistent choices every day, even when the path is difficult. This is where intentional action comes into play, requiring awareness and determination.

Moving from intention to action is central to the ACT approach. The other processes in ACT—such as defusion from negative thoughts, acceptance of difficult emotions, mindful awareness, and the concept of self as context—all support this transition, helping you stay focused and motivated on your journey.

One of the most common obstacles people face is the gap between what they intend to do and what they actually do. Often, this gap is fueled by fear, procrastination, or simply not knowing how to proceed. However, even small steps can make a big difference. It's through continued daily effort that your intentions become a tangible reality.

Not every action needs to be grand. Even small gestures, when aligned with your values, contribute to building an authentic and meaningful life. The key is maintaining consistency between what you consider significant and your daily choices. Remember that every action counts, and over time, these daily choices will shape the course of your life.

Acting in a way that's consistent with your values is what turns your ideals into reality. This process allows you to build a life that not only reflects what's important to you but also gives you the satisfaction of living authentically and meaningfully.

Creating SMART Goals Based on Values

To turn your values into concrete and measurable actions, using SMART goals can be incredibly effective. SMART goals help ensure that your actions are not only intentional but also well-planned and achievable. But what does SMART actually mean? It's an acronym that describes the characteristics a goal should have to be effective: Specific, Measurable, Achievable, Relevant, and Time-bound.

Definition and Application of SMART Goals

1. Specific: A specific goal answers questions like "What do I want to achieve?" and "Why is it important?" Clearly defining what you want to accomplish helps you focus your efforts and map out a precise path. For example, instead of saying "I want to improve my health," a more specific goal could be "I want to lose 5 kilograms in three months to improve my cardiovascular health."

2. Measurable: A goal must be measurable so you can track your progress. This means you need to be able to quantify the outcome you want to achieve. In our example, losing 5 kilograms is a clear and measurable indicator of progress.

3. Achievable: A goal should be realistic and achievable given your resources and limitations. Setting overly ambitious goals can lead to discouragement and quitting. Returning to the weight loss example, setting a goal to lose 5 kilograms in three months is reasonable and achievable for most people with a balanced diet and exercise plan.

4. Relevant: A goal should be relevant and aligned with your abilities and resources. It's important that the goal is meaningful to you and aligns with your values. If one of your values is health, setting a weight loss goal is both realistic and relevant.

5. Time-bound: Finally, a SMART goal should have a deadline. This helps you stay motivated and track your progress. In our example, the three-month deadline provides a clear time frame within which to achieve the desired result.

Aligning SMART Goals with Personal Values

Aligning your SMART goals with your personal values is crucial to ensuring that your actions are consistent with what truly matters to you. This means that each goal you set should reflect the principles and priorities you've identified as central to your life.

To do this, start by asking yourself which values you want to honor. For example, if one of your core values is personal growth, you might set a SMART goal that challenges you to improve a skill or acquire new knowledge. This could be something like "Read one book a month to deepen my understanding of psychology."

Another example could relate to the value of family. If family connection is an important value for you, a SMART goal might be "Organize a family dinner every week to strengthen family bonds and create shared memories." This goal is specific, measurable, achievable, relevant, and has a clear time frame.

Examples of SMART Goals in Different Areas of Life

Let's look at how to apply SMART goals in various areas of your life, ensuring they're always aligned with your values:

1. Health and Well-being: If your value is health, a SMART goal could be "Exercise for 30 minutes five times a week to improve my endurance and mental well-being." This goal is specific (exercise), measurable (30 minutes, five times a week), achievable and realistic for many people, and has a time frame (weekly).

2. Professional Growth: If one of your values is professional development, a SMART goal could be "Complete an online course on time management within the next two months to improve my work efficiency." This goal aligns with the value of growth and possesses all the SMART characteristics.

3. Relationships: If you place great importance on relationships, you might set a SMART goal like "Spend one hour every day, without distractions, focusing on quality time with my partner to strengthen our connection." Again, the goal is specific (quality time), measurable (one hour daily), achievable and realistic, and has a clear time frame (daily).

4. Personal Growth: For a value like personal growth, you might define a SMART goal such as "Journal for 15 minutes every evening to reflect on my day and work on my self-awareness." This goal is specific (journaling), measurable (15 minutes each evening), achievable, realistic, and has a defined time frame (evening).

By applying the SMART model to your goals, you not only increase your chances of success but also ensure that every action is deeply rooted in your values, making your personal growth journey more meaningful and fulfilling.

Overcoming Obstacles to Action

Even with clear goals and strong motivation, it's common to encounter obstacles that can hinder your progress toward actions aligned with your values. These obstacles may come in the form of internal barriers, such as fear of failure or procrastination, or they may stem from external influences that test your resolve. In this section, we'll explore how to identify and overcome these obstacles, using the processes of Acceptance and Commitment Therapy (ACT) to help you stay committed and move forward.

The first step is recognizing the barriers that may prevent you from taking action. These barriers can be both psychological and practical, often manifesting in subtle yet powerful ways. Some of the most common obstacles include:

1. Fear of Failure: The fear of not succeeding can be paralyzing. When you're afraid of failing, you might avoid taking action altogether, preferring the safety of inaction. This fear can stem from unrealistic expectations, fear of judgment from others, or a lack of confidence in your abilities.

2. Procrastination: Putting off important actions, even when you know they matter, is an easy trap to fall into. Procrastination can result from a lack of clarity, feeling overwhelmed by the commitment required, or simply a tendency to avoid discomfort.

3. External Influences: Social pressures, family or work expectations, and even environmental conditions can be significant obstacles. These external factors can cause you to doubt your choices or distract you from your goals.

4. Self-Sabotaging Thoughts: Thoughts like "I'm not good enough," "It's too hard," or "There's no point in trying" can become powerful barriers if you don't recognize and manage them effectively.

Overcoming fear of failure and procrastination requires a combination of awareness, self-compassion, and practical strategies.

1. Accepting Fear: Fear of failure is natural, but it doesn't have to be an insurmountable obstacle. A helpful approach is to accept fear as part of the process. Recognize that fear is a signal you're stepping out of your comfort zone, which is often necessary for growth. Instead of fighting it, learn to coexist with this emotion while continuing to move toward your goals.

2. Focusing on the Process, Not Just the Outcome: Often, fear of failure is rooted in the belief that the end result is all that matters. However, if you focus on the process and the small steps you can take each day, you reduce the pressure you place on yourself. This allows you to see value in every action, regardless of the final outcome.

3. Breaking Down Goals: Procrastination can be tackled by breaking a task down into smaller, manageable parts. Instead of viewing a goal as one massive, daunting task, divide it into simpler actions. This makes it easier to start and helps you build momentum as you complete each step.

4. Commitment and Self-Compassion: It's important to remember that you don't have to be perfect. Commit to doing your best, but treat yourself kindly when things don't go as planned. Self-compassion allows you to face obstacles without judgment, reducing performance anxiety and increasing your resilience.

Using Other ACT Processes to Overcome Obstacles

The ACT processes offer powerful tools for overcoming the barriers that can hinder committed action. Here's how you can use some of these processes:

1. Defusion from Negative Thoughts: Defusion helps you create distance from thoughts that hold you back. When you notice a self-sabotaging thought, such as "I can't do this," practice defusion by recognizing that it's just a thought, not a reality. This allows you to avoid identifying with your thoughts and continue to act despite them.

2. Acceptance of Difficult Emotions: Accepting difficult emotions, such as fear or frustration, is crucial for staying committed. Acceptance doesn't mean giving in, but rather allowing emotions to exist without letting them dictate your actions. Embracing these emotions with openness enables you to stay focused on your values, even when emotions run high.

3. Mindful Presence: Staying in the present moment helps you avoid being overwhelmed by fears of the future or regrets about the past. Mindfulness allows you to tackle one task at a time, with attention and intention, reducing anxiety and improving the quality of your actions.

4. Commitment to Values: Finally, continually reminding yourself of the values that guide your actions can give you the motivation needed to overcome obstacles. When faced with a challenge, ask yourself how this action reflects your core values. This helps you stay grounded in what truly matters and find the strength to keep going.

Overcoming obstacles to action requires time, patience, and practice, but with the right tools and an open mindset, it's possible to face and overcome the challenges you encounter along your path. By consciously using ACT strategies, you can maintain your commitment to a life that fully reflects your values, viewing each obstacle as an opportunity for growth.

Developing Persistence and Resilience

When it comes to pursuing your goals and living according to your values, it's not just about starting with enthusiasm; it's the ability to stay the course that truly makes a difference. This ability is built through persistence and resilience, two essential qualities that help you remain steady in the face of difficulties and changes. In this section, we'll explore how to cultivate these qualities to tackle challenges and maintain long-term motivation.

Persistence is what allows you to keep making progress, even when the journey gets tough. It's easy to be motivated at the beginning, but over time, enthusiasm can wane, especially when results aren't immediate or obstacles seem insurmountable. In these moments, persistence becomes crucial: it's about taking one step at a time without getting discouraged by setbacks. Even when progress seems slow or insignificant, every small step brings you closer to your goals.

Being persistent doesn't just mean continuing to do the same things but adapting and finding new ways to tackle difficulties. The path to success is never linear, and being able to stay flexible helps you overcome crises. Instead of seeing difficulties as insurmountable barriers, you can start to view them as opportunities to learn and grow. This change in perspective is the foundation of resilience.

Resilience, in fact, is the ability to adapt and bounce back in the face of adversity. It's not just about enduring difficulties but using them as leverage to improve and move forward. Building resilience means developing the ability to stay calm under pressure, see problems in a broader context, and find creative solutions even in the most complicated situations.

To build resilience, it can be helpful to review how you perceive difficulties. Every challenge you encounter can be an opportunity to better understand yourself, refine your strategies, and approach your goals in ways you hadn't considered before. This approach helps you turn adversities into growth moments rather than just seeing them as obstacles.

Another key element in developing persistence and resilience is maintaining high motivation, especially in the long term. Motivation isn't an infinite resource; it's normal for it to fluctuate. However, there are ways to keep it consistently fueled. For example, setting small milestones and rewarding yourself when you reach them can help keep your energy alive. Even simply acknowledging your effort can do a lot to strengthen your motivation.

It's also important to periodically review your goals. Life changes, and with it, your priorities and values may also change. Reviewing your goals and ensuring they are still aligned with what's truly important to you can give you a new push. This helps you stay focused and avoid the frustration that can come from pursuing goals that no longer represent you.

Cultivating gratitude can be a powerful source of motivation. Take time to reflect on what you've already achieved and what you're grateful for. This not only helps you maintain a positive perspective but also reminds you of why you started this journey. When you're feeling down or discouraged, remembering your past successes and the positive things in your life can give you the energy you need to keep going.

Exercise 1: Creating SMART Goals

Start by identifying a key value that is important to you. Using this value as your guide, define a SMART goal: Specific, Measurable, Achievable, Relevant, and Time-bound. Then, plan the specific actions you will take to achieve this goal.

Key Value (Briefly describe one of your core values):

_____

_____

SMART Goal:

Specific:
(What exactly do you want to achieve? Describe it clearly and precisely.)

_____

_____

Measurable:
(How will you measure your progress? What indicators will you use to know if you are moving toward your goal?)

_____

_____

Achievable:
(Is this goal realistic given your resources and limitations? If needed, what additional resources will you require?)

_____

_____

Relevant:
(Is your goal relevant and aligned with your abilities and priorities? Why is it important to you?)

_____

_____

Time-bound:
(By when do you want to achieve this goal? Set a clear and realistic deadline.)

_____

_____

Action Plan:

Action 1:

(Describe the first concrete action you can take.)

_____

_____

_____

Action 2:

(Describe a second concrete action.)

_____

_____

_____

Action 3:

(Describe a third concrete action, if needed.)

_____

_____

_____

Final Reflection: How will you feel when you achieve this goal? What obstacles might arise, and how will you overcome them?

_____

_____

_____

_____

_____

Exercise 2: Overcoming Obstacles

Think about an important action that aligns with your values but that you've been avoiding. Describe the action, the obstacles that have prevented you from taking it, and finally, create a detailed plan to overcome these obstacles.

Important Action:

(Briefly describe the action you've been avoiding.)

_____

_____

_____

Obstacles Encountered:

(List and describe the obstacles that have held you back.)

_____

_____

_____

Plan to Overcome Obstacles:

(Detail how you will tackle and overcome these obstacles. Outline concrete steps you can take.)

_____

_____

_____

_____

_____

_____

_____

Exercise 3: Committed Action Journal

For the next 5 days, record a daily action you've taken that aligns with your values, even if it's a small one. This will help you reflect on how you are putting your values into practice in your everyday life.

Date	Action	Related Value	Reflections

Chapter 25:

ACT for Anxiety and Depression

"You don't have to control your thoughts. You just have to stop letting them control you."
- Dan Millman

In this chapter, we will explore how Acceptance and Commitment Therapy can be effectively applied to address anxiety and depression, two of the most common and debilitating psychological disorders. ACT does not aim to completely eliminate anxiety or depression, but rather to change how we relate to these internal experiences, allowing us to live a richer and more meaningful life despite the presence of these challenges.

Applying ACT to anxiety disorders

Imagine anxiety not as an enemy to fight, but as a part of you, a travel companion you didn't choose, but with whom you can learn to coexist. Instead of desperately trying to control or eliminate it, what if you tried simply accepting it? This is the central idea of Acceptance and Commitment Therapy (ACT): anxiety isn't something to be defeated, but an experience we can embrace while continuing to live a meaningful life.

But how can we do this? Often, when we experience anxiety, we tend to believe our thoughts are absolute, undeniable truths. If we think, "I'll never be able to do this," it's easy to fall into the trap of truly believing it, as if it were carved in stone. ACT teaches us to take a step back and see these thoughts for what they are: simple products of our mind. They are not absolute truths, but just thoughts.

Consider this example: you're faced with a situation that triggers your anxiety, like public speaking. Your mind might tell you, "I won't be able to do this, everyone will think I'm ridiculous." Instead of accepting this thought as fact, ACT encourages you to recognize it for what it is: a thought. You might say to yourself, "I'm having the thought that I won't be able to do this." In this way, you separate yourself from the thought and reduce its power over you.

And then there's the question of values. What is truly important to you? Perhaps, despite the anxiety, you deeply desire to connect with others, share ideas, or simply live a full life. When we focus on our values, we can find the motivation to act despite anxiety. This doesn't mean the anxiety will disappear, but that we will learn to move through it, guided by what truly matters.

A practical example might be this: you're afraid of attending a social event, but you know that human connection is a central value for you. ACT encourages you to acknowledge the anxiety, make space for it within yourself, and attend the event anyway, because you know it aligns with your values. It's a way of telling your anxiety, "I know you're here, but I have important things to do."

To effectively deal with anxiety, it's helpful to understand the concept of expansion. Imagine anxiety as a feeling of tightness or pressure in your chest. The natural reaction is to want to escape or make it go away. But what would happen if, instead of shrinking away, you tried to "expand" around that anxiety?

Expansion is a technique that teaches us to create a space within ourselves where anxiety can exist without overwhelming us. Practically, this means observing the anxiety and its physical manifestations, like muscle tension or rapid breathing, without trying to change or avoid them. Imagine taking a deep breath and visualizing your body as a container that expands, capable of holding that anxiety without bursting. This approach allows anxiety to be present without limiting us, leaving us free to act in line with our values.

Mindfulness also plays a crucial role in managing anxiety. By staying present in the moment, we can reduce the tendency to ruminate on what has happened or worry about what might happen. With mindfulness, we focus on what we can do here and now, keeping our attention on what is within our control.

Ultimately, ACT teaches us that anxiety doesn't have to stop us from living a full and meaningful life. We don't have to wait for anxiety to disappear to start living. We can choose to act in line with our values, even if anxiety is present. This is the true freedom that ACT offers: the ability to be ourselves, despite everything.

ACT in Managing Depression

Depression often manifests as a heaviness that permeates every aspect of life, turning even the simplest tasks into insurmountable challenges. In this condition, ACT offers an approach that doesn't focus solely on eliminating symptoms, but rather on changing the way we relate to them. The goal is not merely to reduce pain, but to live a life that is meaningful, even in the presence of suffering.

A key characteristic of depression is the entrapment in repetitive negative thoughts. These thoughts, often internalized as unchangeable truths, can claim things like "My life has no meaning" or "Things will only get worse." However, ACT invites us to distance ourselves from these thoughts. Instead of accepting them as definitive realities, it encourages us to see them for what they really are: products of the mind, not concrete facts. This ability to cognitively defuse allows us to observe these thoughts with a certain detachment, reducing their influence and opening the door to new possibilities for action.

Consider the loss of interest that often accompanies depression. Activities that once brought joy or meaning become devoid of appeal, leaving us in a state of apathy. This is where ACT's concept of committed action comes into play. Even when everything seems meaningless, ACT encourages us to continue taking actions that reflect our deepest values. It's not about waiting to feel motivated or inspired, but about acting because these actions align with what we hold important, even if depression pushes us to do the opposite.

For example, if connection with others is a central value in your life, but depression isolates you, ACT encourages you to take a small step, like sending a message to a friend or going out for a brief meeting. These small steps, even though difficult, represent a movement toward a more meaningful life.

Depression tends to anchor us in the past, making us relive mistakes and failures, or project us into a future that we perceive as hopeless. Mindfulness, which we've seen as a fundamental component of ACT, brings us back to the present, allowing us to live in the here and now. This doesn't mean ignoring the pain, but rather allowing ourselves to be aware of what is happening in this very moment, without judgment. Being present can offer a break from the continuous cycle of depressive thoughts, providing a moment of respite where a bit of peace can be found.

In conclusion, ACT proposes a different way of managing depression—not by trying to eliminate it, but by integrating it into a life lived according to our values. Through cognitive defusion, committed action, and mindfulness, we can create a space where depression does not define who we are, allowing us to live with authenticity and meaning, even in the face of difficulties.

ACT and Self-Compassion

When dealing with anxiety and depression, one of the most common obstacles is how you treat yourself during these difficult times. Often, you tend to judge yourself harshly for experiencing these emotions, seeing them as signs of weakness or personal failure. This kind of self-criticism only intensifies your pain and can make the healing process even more challenging. That's why it's important to practice and understand self-compassion.

But what does it really mean to have compassion for yourself? It's easy to misunderstand this concept, confusing it with self-pity or a way to avoid responsibility. In reality, self-compassion is an attitude that requires strength and courage. It means recognizing your own suffering and responding to it with kindness, rather than judgment. It's not about indulging in your negative feelings, but accepting that these are part of the human experience, treating yourself with the same care and understanding you would offer a loved one.

There are several common myths that often lead to misunderstandings about self-compassion. Debunking these myths can help you better understand the importance of this attitude:

1. "Self-Compassion is a Form of Weakness": Many believe that treating yourself gently means being weak or not facing your problems. In reality, self-compassion requires great courage because it involves accepting your vulnerability and the willingness to face difficulties with an open heart, rather than with harshness.

2. "Being Self-Compassionate Means Being Self-Indulgent": There's a false belief that self-compassion is an excuse to avoid taking responsibility or improving yourself. However, compassion doesn't mean justifying harmful behaviors or accepting inertia. On the contrary, it encourages you to recognize your mistakes without judging yourself, allowing you to grow and improve from a position of self-love and respect.

3. "Self-Compassion Leads to Self-Pity": Another myth is that self-compassion leads to complaining about your problems without doing anything to solve them. True compassion, however, motivates you to face challenges with a positive and constructive attitude, rather than falling into the trap of self-pity.

4. "Self-Compassion is Selfish": Some people believe that focusing on yourself in this way is selfish. However, developing self-compassion makes you more capable of being compassionate and available to others. When you treat yourself kindly, you're less likely to project your frustrations onto others and more able to offer support.

Self-compassion is based on three main elements, which together form a complete and powerful practice:

1. Self-Kindness: Instead of criticizing yourself harshly for your difficulties or mistakes, try to respond with gentleness. This doesn't mean justifying your mistakes, but recognizing that we are all imperfect human beings and that failure and suffering are part of life.

2. Common Humanity: Self-compassion reminds you that you're not alone in your sufferings. Everyone goes through difficult times, and recognizing that suffering is a common part of the human experience can reduce the sense of isolation that often accompanies anxiety and depression.

3. Mindfulness: Mindfulness is essential for self-compassion because it allows you to observe your thoughts and feelings without judging them. With mindfulness, you can recognize your pain without completely identifying with it, creating a space for acceptance and kindness.

This perspective allows you to create a space of acceptance where suffering can be observed without being amplified by self-criticism. Self-compassion is not an act of weakness, but a fundamental step towards greater resilience and well-being.

A practical approach to cultivating self-compassion can begin with identifying your self-critical thoughts. Often, when you're anxious or depressed, you tell yourself things like "My life is meaningless" or "I can't go on anymore". These thoughts can become a cycle of negativity that further fuels your distress.

ACT encourages you to recognize these thoughts and respond to them with kindness. A useful exercise is to imagine what you would say to a friend going through your same situation. You probably wouldn't criticize them, but would try to comfort them, acknowledging the difficulty of the moment and offering support. You should apply the same attitude to yourself.

Self-compassion also extends to your emotional response. When you feel anxiety or depression, your instinctive reaction may be to reject or fight them. However, as we've seen, ACT suggests a different approach: making room for these emotions, accepting them as part of your human experience. By treating them with compassion, you can alleviate the associated emotional burden and reduce the resistance that often exacerbates suffering.

In practice, you might try dedicating a few minutes each day to a brief meditation on self-compassion. It might be helpful to sit in a quiet place, close your eyes, and mentally repeat phrases like "May I be kind to myself", "May I accept my emotions as they are", or "May I treat myself with the same compassion I reserve for others". This type of meditation can help you root self-compassion as a mental habit, transforming the way you relate to your internal experiences.

Exercise 1: Defusion from Anxious/Depressive Thoughts

Identify three recurring thoughts related to anxiety or depression. For each thought, write a defusion phrase that helps you distance yourself from it.

Original Thought	Defusion Phrase

Exercise 2: Value-Aligned Action

Choose a value that is important to you, such as family, honesty, or health. Plan 4 small actions aligned with this value that you could take when you feel anxious or depressed. These actions will help you stay connected to your values, even during difficult times.

Chosen Value:

Action 1:

_____

_____

_____

Action 2:

_____

_____

_____

Action 3:

_____

_____

_____

Action 4:

_____

_____

_____

Exercise 3: Self-Compassion Practice

Write a brief letter of compassion to yourself, as if you were speaking to a dear friend who is struggling with anxiety or depression. This letter should reflect kindness, understanding, and support, acknowledging the difficulties you are facing without judgment.

Chapter 26:

ACT in Relationships and Work

"The quality of your life is the quality of your relationships." - Tony Robbins

In this chapter, we will explore how Acceptance and Commitment Therapy can be applied to significantly improve our interpersonal relationships and work life. We will see how ACT principles can transform our daily interactions, help us manage work-related stress and burnout, and enhance our communication.

Improving Relationships Through ACT

Interpersonal relationships are at the core of our human experience, but they can also be a source of significant challenges and difficulties. Acceptance and Commitment Therapy offers an innovative approach to enhancing the quality of our interactions, based on its fundamental principles of acceptance, cognitive defusion, present moment awareness, values, and committed action. Applying ACT Processes in Interpersonal Interactions:

1. Acceptance: In relationships, acceptance involves recognizing that the other person has thoughts, emotions, and behaviors that may differ from our own. Instead of trying to change the other person or reacting negatively to these differences, ACT encourages us to accept these diversities as a natural part of human relationships. This doesn't mean tolerating harmful behavior, but rather creating a space for mutual understanding and respect.

2. Cognitive Defusion: Conflicts in relationships often arise from rigid interpretations of others' behaviors. Defusion helps us step back from our automatic thoughts and the labels we apply to others. For example, instead of thinking, "They are always so selfish," we might say to ourselves, "I am having the thought that they are selfish." This creates space for a deeper and less reactive understanding.

3. Present Moment Awareness: Being fully present in our interactions significantly enhances the quality of our relationships. Practicing mindfulness during conversations allows us to listen more attentively, pick up on non-verbal cues, and respond in a more authentic and compassionate manner.

4. Self as Context: This process helps us see ourselves and others beyond the roles and labels we tend to apply. Recognizing that we are more than our actions or mistakes can lead to greater empathy and understanding in relationships.

5. Values: Identifying and living according to our relational values can guide us in difficult situations. If we value compassion, we can choose to respond kindly even when we are frustrated. If honesty is a key value, we can commit to communicating openly, even when it is uncomfortable.

6. Committed Action: This process encourages us to take concrete steps to improve our relationships, even when we feel vulnerable or uncertain. This might mean starting a difficult conversation, offering an apology, or taking the first step toward reconciliation.

How Psychological Flexibility Can Improve Communication:

Psychological flexibility is essential for effective communication. It allows us to adapt to different relational situations, respond more appropriately to the needs of the moment, and manage conflicts constructively. For example:

- We can shift from active listening to assertive expression when necessary.

- We are able to recognize when our thoughts or emotions are negatively affecting communication and take a step back.

- We can adapt our communication style based on the person we are interacting with, while still maintaining our authenticity.

Using Values to Guide Decisions in Relationships: Personal values can serve as a compass in our relationships, helping us make decisions that align with what truly matters to us. Some examples include:

- If we value personal growth, we might choose to view conflicts as learning opportunities rather than threats.

- If intimacy is a key value, we might prioritize quality time with our partner, even when we are busy.

- If we appreciate authenticity, we might choose to express our feelings honestly, even when it's uncomfortable.

Applying ACT in the Workplace

Work can be a source of satisfaction, but it can also bring stress and challenges. You spend a significant part of your life at work, so it's natural to sometimes feel overwhelmed by pressures, deadlines, and relationships with colleagues. This is where Acceptance and Commitment Therapy (ACT) can make a difference, offering practical tools to help you navigate workplace challenges with greater calm and effectiveness.

At work, it's easy to fall into the trap of trying to control every aspect of your day, from the emotions you feel to the outcomes you achieve. However, ACT teaches you that you don't have to fight against every negative thought or feeling that arises. Instead of trying to suppress the anxiety you might feel before an important presentation, you can learn to recognize it, accept it, and then take action anyway, with the courage that comes from knowing that anxiety doesn't have to define or stop you.

In work, as in life, change is inevitable. It could be a company restructuring, a change in role, or a project taking an unexpected direction. These changes can create uncertainty, but ACT encourages you to face them with an open mind, embracing change as an opportunity for growth and learning. You don't have to view every shift as a threat; rather, you can see it as a natural part of your professional journey.

Workplace relationships can be complex. You might find yourself at odds with a colleague or frustrated by negative feedback. In these situations, ACT invites you to take a step back and avoid reacting impulsively. Instead of being swept up by the emotions of the moment, you can learn to observe your thoughts, create some distance, and respond in a more thoughtful and constructive way. This approach not only improves the quality of your interactions but also helps maintain a more harmonious work environment.

In the workplace, it's easy to lose sight of what truly matters to you. Daily pressures and urgent demands can push your values and long-term goals to the background. ACT offers you the opportunity to reconnect with what is truly important to you, helping you make decisions that reflect your core values. Perhaps professional growth is essential to you, meaning you need to dedicate time to developing new skills, even when your workload already feels overwhelming. Or maybe your integrity guides you, leading you to choose transparency in your communications, even when it might seem easier to hide the truth.

At the end of the day, what matters isn't just how much you've worked or how many tasks you've completed, but whether you've done it in a way that's consistent with who you are and who you want to become. Applying ACT in your work helps you stay focused on what truly matters, manage stress more effectively, and build a career that not only satisfies you but also reflects your deepest values and aspirations.

Practical Tips for Applying ACT at Work:

- Accept that stress is a part of work, and don't try to avoid it at all costs.

- Practice mindfulness during breaks to mentally recharge.

- When a negative thought arises, acknowledge it as such and don't let it influence your actions.

- Focus on what you can control and let go of what is beyond your control.

- Align your work decisions with your values to maintain a sense of integrity.

- View every change as an opportunity to learn and grow, not as a threat.

- Communicate clearly and honestly, even when it's difficult, to build trust.

- Take a few minutes at the end of the day to reflect on what went well, without judging yourself for mistakes.

- Maintain a flexible mindset, adapting to new tasks or sudden requests.

- Set realistic and achievable goals to avoid mental overload.

- Be kind to yourself when things don't go as planned; learning from mistakes is essential.

- Use criticism as a tool for growth, rather than as confirmation of inadequacy.

- Take short breaks to reduce mental overload and stay focused.

- Try to cultivate positive relationships with colleagues to create a more harmonious work environment.

- When you feel overwhelmed, remember that it's normal and focus on taking one step at a time.

Managing Stress and Burnout

Stress is the body's natural response to any demand or pressure. When you're facing an imminent deadline, an important presentation, or a significant change, your body goes into a state of alert. This state, known as "fight or flight," prepares your body to react quickly, increasing your heart rate, muscle tension, and mental alertness. In small doses, this state can be helpful, giving you the energy needed to tackle a challenge.

However, when stress becomes a constant presence in your life, your body remains in a continuous state of alert without ever having the chance to relax. This chronic stress can lead to various health problems, including heart disease, insomnia, depression, anxiety, and digestive issues. Additionally, stress negatively impacts your cognitive abilities, reducing your concentration, memory, and problem-solving skills.

Burnout, on the other hand, is a severe form of physical, emotional, and mental exhaustion caused by prolonged stress. It's not just about feeling tired or temporarily drained; burnout is a state where you feel completely depleted, disconnected from your work, and unable to handle even the simplest daily tasks. Signs of burnout include cynicism, emotional detachment, a sense of inefficacy, and decreased productivity.

While stress can make you feel overly involved in your activities, burnout makes you feel the opposite: detached, disinterested, and lacking motivation. It's important to recognize that burnout isn't just a matter of overwork but also a lack of balance and connection with what you do. Often, burnout results from a misalignment between what is important to you and what you do every day.

The causes of stress and burnout can vary widely from person to person, but some common factors tend to contribute to these issues:

- Excessive workload: When you constantly feel overwhelmed by work demands without enough time to complete tasks, the risk of stress and burnout increases significantly.

- Lack of control: Feeling powerless or unable to influence decisions related to your work can be a major cause of stress. The lack of autonomy can lead to feelings of frustration and helplessness.

- Unclear expectations: If you're unsure about what is expected of you, or if expectations frequently change without clear communication, it's easy to feel disoriented and stressed.

- Disconnection from personal values: When your work doesn't reflect your values or what you find important, it's easy to lose motivation and slip into burnout.

- Lack of social support: An isolated or conflictual work environment can increase stress and accelerate the burnout process.

Addressing stress and preventing burnout requires an integrated approach that considers both physical and mental well-being. Here are some strategies that can help:

- Set clear boundaries: Learn to say no when necessary and establish clear distinctions between work and personal life. Ensure you have time for yourself, away from work responsibilities.

- Practice self-care: Get enough sleep, eat a balanced diet, and exercise regularly. These three pillars of physical health also support your ability to manage stress.

- Manage time effectively: Use time management techniques, such as task planning or the Pomodoro technique, to avoid feeling overwhelmed.

- Cultivate positive relationships: Supportive relationships both inside and outside of work can provide crucial emotional support. Talk to colleagues, friends, or family when you feel stressed.

- Take regular breaks: Don't underestimate the importance of breaks during the workday. Even a few minutes can help you recharge and maintain focus.

- Reconnect with your values: Reflect on what truly matters to you and strive to align your work with these values. This will help sustain motivation and prevent burnout.

- Delegate tasks: Don't try to do everything yourself. Delegating tasks and responsibilities can ease your workload and prevent overload.

- Consider workload adjustments: If you feel overwhelmed, discuss with your supervisor the possibility of temporarily reducing your workload.

- Take time off when needed: If stress becomes overwhelming, consider taking some time off to recharge.

Values-Based Communication

Effective communication is the foundation of any successful work relationship. Whether you're interacting with colleagues, managers, clients, or collaborators, the ability to communicate clearly and assertively can make the difference between a productive day and one filled with misunderstandings. However, communication isn't just about conveying information; it's also a reflection of who you are and what you hold important. This is where the concept of values-based communication comes into play.

What is Values-Based Communication?

Values-based communication means expressing yourself in a way that your words and actions reflect your core principles. When you communicate according to your values, you're not just delivering a message; you're doing so in a way that resonates with who you truly are and what matters to you. This type of communication is authentic, consistent, and often more effective because it is perceived as genuine and sincere.

For example, if one of your core values is transparency, your communication will likely be clear and straightforward. You won't just say what others want to hear; you'll strive to share information honestly, even when it's challenging. If you value collaboration, you'll seek to include others' opinions in discussions, showing respect and openness.

Values-based communication is important because it builds trust and credibility. When people perceive that you communicate consistently with your values, they are more likely to trust you. This can significantly improve workplace dynamics, facilitating collaboration and reducing conflicts. Moreover, this type of communication helps you feel more aligned with yourself, reducing the stress that can come from saying or doing things that don't reflect who you truly are.

Another key aspect of values-based communication is that it allows you to handle difficult situations with greater integrity. When you need to give critical feedback or address a conflict, speaking from your values enables you to do so in a respectful and constructive manner. This not only improves the quality of interactions but also helps maintain a positive and productive work environment.

The first step in practicing values-based communication is to clearly identify your core values. These might include honesty, kindness, respect, responsibility, or empathy. Once you've identified your values, you can start reflecting on how you want them to be reflected in the way you communicate with others.

Here are some concrete steps you can take:

- Reflect before you act: Before any important conversation, take a moment to think about the values you want to embody. This will help you stay calm and communicate clearly, especially in delicate situations.

- Choose your words carefully: The words you use are a reflection of your values. When communicating, make sure your language truly represents who you are. Avoid expressions that might exclude or diminish others, especially if you value collaboration.

- Practice active listening: Communication isn't just about talking; it's also about listening. If you value empathy, demonstrate it by listening attentively to others without interrupting or judging. Genuine listening strengthens trust and mutual openness.

- Align words and actions: Consistency between what you say and what you do is crucial. Your body language and tone of voice should be in harmony with your values. For instance, if you promote openness, ensure that your behavior doesn't convey defensiveness or closed-mindedness.

- Handle conflicts with respect: When dealing with conflict, let your values guide your response. Acting with integrity and respect can turn a confrontation into a growth opportunity for both parties, avoiding aggressive or passive reactions.

- Seek honest feedback: Don't hesitate to ask for feedback on your communication. This will help you understand whether others perceive your consistency and authenticity, giving you the chance to continuously improve.

- Be patient with yourself: Perfecting values-based communication takes time and practice. If you don't always express yourself as you'd like, don't be discouraged. Every conversation is an opportunity to learn and refine your skills.

Exercise 1: Values in Relationships

Identify three values that are important to you in your personal and professional relationships. For each value, describe a specific action you could take to live that value more fully in your daily interactions.

Value 1:

Action:

Value 2:

Action:

Value 3:

Action:

Exercise 2: Mindfulness at Work

Plan how to incorporate brief moments of mindfulness into your workday. Identify three specific times during the day and describe a short mindfulness practice you can do during those moments.

Time of day:

Mindfulness practice:

Time of day:

Mindfulness practice:

Time of day:

Mindfulness practice:

Exercise 3: Values-Based Communication

Think of a difficult conversation you need to have soon. Using ACT principles, plan how you will handle this conversation assertively and in alignment with your values. Describe the situation, identify the relevant values, list the key points you want to communicate, and outline the ACT strategies you will use.

Description of the situation

_____

_____

_____

_____

_____

Relevant values:

_____

_____

_____

_____

Key points to communicate:

_____

_____

_____

_____

_____

_____

Your Insights

"The greatest good you can do for another is not just to share your riches but to reveal to him his own." — Benjamin Disraeli

As you close this workbook, reflect on your journey through DBT, CBT, and ACT techniques. The strategies you've learned and the insights you've gained are not just personal achievements—they have the power to inspire and guide others.

Consider this: Would you be willing to help someone you've never met, at no cost to yourself, even if you received no recognition for it?

If your answer is yes, here's how you can make a difference:

Someone out there is where you were before opening this book—seeking ways to manage depression, anxiety, or improve their mental health. Your honest review could be the guiding light they need to find this resource.

By sharing your experience, you can:

- Help someone discover effective mental health strategies
- Encourage another person to take the first step towards healing
- Contribute to breaking the stigma surrounding mental health

Your feedback, whether highlighting strengths or offering constructive criticism, is invaluable. It takes less than five minutes but could change someone's life.

I appreciate all reviews and read each one personally. Your insights help improve future resources and support others on their mental health journey.

Ready to make a difference?

Thank you for your time and for being part of this supportive community.

With gratitude, Isabelle Rivers

Scan to leave a review on Amazon if you live in the US

Scan to leave a review on Amazon if you live in the UK

Scan to leave a review on Amazon if you live in Canada

Scan to leave a review on Amazon if you live in Australia

A New Beginning, Not an End

Dear reader,

You've reached the last page of this book, but in reality, this is just the beginning. The journey you've taken through these pages is as unique as you are. As you close this book, I want you to know one thing: I'm incredibly proud of you.

You might be thinking, "But you don't even know me." True, we've never met in person, but through these pages, we've shared something profound. I've seen your strength in deciding to open this book, your perseverance in reading each page, and your courage in facing the challenges life has thrown at you.

Remember when we talked about mindfulness? About how being present in the moment can change your perspective? Well, this is one of those moments. Take a pause. Breathe deeply. Feel the weight of the book in your hands, observe the thoughts crossing your mind right now. This awareness, this presence, is the first step towards the change you desire.

The DBT, CBT, and ACT techniques we've explored together aren't just tools: they're bridges. Bridges connecting the you of today to the you of tomorrow, that version of yourself you've always known you could be. Every time you use cognitive restructuring to challenge a negative thought, every time you practice emotional regulation in a moment of stress, you're building that bridge, one piece at a time.

I know there will be days when it seems difficult. Days when old habits feel stronger than new intentions. In those moments, remember this: change isn't an event, it's a process. And in that process, you're not alone.

Here's what I ask of you now:

- Choose one technique, just one, from those we've discussed. The one that made you think, "Yes, this could work for me." Commit to practicing it every day for the next week. It doesn't have to be perfect, it just needs to be consistent.
- At the end of this week, write a letter to yourself. Tell yourself how you felt, what you noticed, what challenges you faced. This letter will be your personal reminder of the journey you've embarked upon.

Remember, behavioral and cognitive therapy isn't about achieving perfection, but about continuous progress. Every small step counts. Every moment of awareness is a victory. Every time you choose to be kind to yourself, you're changing your world.

As you close this book, I want you to know that I believe in you. In your potential for growth, in your ability to face challenges, in your inner strength that perhaps you haven't fully realized yet.

The journey continues, and I'm honored to have been part of your path, even if only through these pages. Always remember: you're stronger than you think, more resilient than you believe, and absolutely capable of creating the life you desire.

With affection and faith in your journey,

Isabelle Rivers

P.S. If you ever feel lost or need a reminder, come back to these pages. They'll always be here for you, just like the spirit of strength and hope you've cultivated during this reading.

About the Author

A respected consultant in the field of mental wellness, Isabelle Rivers has helped numerous individuals overcome emotional challenges and enjoy more fulfilling lives. Her expertise extends beyond individual therapy to assisting those navigating difficult periods or life transitions, supporting their recovery and preparing them for new challenges.

Driven by a desire to share her experiences and knowledge with a broader audience, particularly those without direct access to therapy, Rivers turned to writing. Her books offer practical, accessible strategies for managing stress, anxiety, and depression, while also providing techniques to improve communication, self-esteem, and interpersonal relationships.

The aim of Rivers' writing is to democratize access to behavioral and cognitive therapy techniques, presenting them in an easily understandable format that readers can apply to their daily lives. Combining scientific rigor with compassion and understanding, her approach reflects extensive experience in addressing a wide range of mental health challenges.

With a firm belief that the right tools and adequate support can significantly improve anyone's emotional well-being and quality of life, Rivers continues to divide her time between writing, consulting, and conducting workshops. Her ongoing mission is to explore new ways of reaching and helping more people on their journey towards better mental health.

www.ingramcontent.com/pod-product-compliance
Lightning Source LLC
Chambersburg PA
CBHW080608270326
41928CB00016B/2969